Praise for
BECOMING MORE

"TOO OFTEN WE SETTLE for far less than God's best for our lives— which is why I'm so excited about *Becoming More*. Dianna Kokoszka has distilled her leadership experience, business success, and personal faith into a powerful catalyst for breaking free from the perceived limitations we place on ourselves. As timeless as it is urgently relevant, *Becoming More* ignites positive change that endures."

—*Chris Hodges*, SENIOR PASTOR,
CHURCH OF THE HIGHLANDS AND
AUTHOR OF OUT OF THE CAVE AND PRAY FIRST

"TO REACH YOUR POTENTIAL, and become the person you were created to be, you must grow. Dianna Kokoszka's *Becoming More* will serve as a road map, helping guide you to a more brilliant future."

—*Mark Cole*, OWNER/CEO OF MAXWELL LEADERSHIP

"IN LOOKING AT THE BECOMING MORE MODEL, we love that Dianna first walked it out and refined it through her own life experience and now brings it to us in a simple, practical, and applicable process. This book is an answer to the powerful future probing question, 'What story do I want to tell with my life?' Start your journey now with Dianna."

—*John Vereecken*, PRESIDENT OF MAXWELL LEADERSHIP ESPAÑOL
AND AUTHOR OF CORAZON DE CAMPEÓN,
AND *Karla Vereecken*,
CONSULTANT FOR MAXWELL LEADERSHIP ESPAÑOL

"THERE ARE NO WORDS for what I have been able to do through Dianna's focus and intellect. She has given the world a remarkable road map to create a positive difference. Her teachings unveil the different steps that will bring us all to live a better story. The knowledge she shares in this book is life-changing."

—*Mary Tennant, FORMER PRESIDENT OF KELLER WILLIAMS REALTY INTERNATIONAL, INVESTOR, AND PHILANTHROPIST*

BECOMING
MORE

BECOMING
MORE

YOU CAN'T GET TO BETTER
UNTIL YOU GET TO DIFFERENT

Dianna Kokoszka

FOREWORD BY JOHN C. MAXWELL

MAXWELL
LEADERSHIP

Published by Maxwell Leadership Publishing,
an imprint of Forefront Books.
Distributed by Simon & Schuster.

Library of Congress Control Number: 2023911884

Print ISBN: 979-8887100067
E-book ISBN: 979-8887100074

Cover Design by Nicole d'Aquin
Interior Design by Mary Susan Oleson, BLU Design Concepts

DEDICATED TO my brother Larry and sister Patsy who, through their struggles and hardships, inspired me to explore the incredible potential of the human brain and our ability to shape our lives through conscious choice. Your legacy lives on.

To my family for the impact and power of their love.

CONTENTS

FOREWORD

You will not find a brighter light than Dianna Kokoszka. Dianna and I have traveled the world together, enjoying many unique experiences over our twenty-five-year friendship. There are two things about her that shine no matter the circumstance: she's always smiling and always learning. Her attitude and passion to continually grow set her apart from the pack. The most successful leaders, and the ones I want to learn from, understand there is no finish line to growth. That's Dianna.

When Dianna told me about writing this book, I remember feeling a strong sense of excitement for you, the reader. You are going to love learning from her!

Becoming More is a guidebook for personal growth. It will serve as your compass to guide you to a better story and leave a legacy that you're proud of.

It was Robert Louis Stevenson who said, "To be what we are and to become what we are capable of becoming is the only end of life." As you read Dianna's words, you will see her heart jumping off the pages. Her desire is to help you become what you are capable of becoming. And I believe she is just the leader for the job.

Growth isn't automatic. It doesn't just happen. Early in my career, I was asked a question I had never been asked before by one of my mentors, Curt Kampmeier. I remember it like it was yesterday. He looked across the table and simply asked, "John, what is your plan for personal growth?" That question became the catalyst for discovering the path to reach my potential.

My growth journey from where I began has often been uncomfortable. It's not pleasant to face where you fall short. It's difficult to leave the familiar in order to grow. But growth comes only as a result of dropping bad habits, changing wrong priorities, and embracing new ways of thinking. People who do not grow cling to the familiar and don't improve. They won't face what is wrong so they can discover what is right.

Growth is an inside job. It's about becoming bigger on the inside than the outside. And that's what I love most about this book. Dianna has gathered all her experiences and lessons together and crafted proven models and practical applications that you can apply to your own life and leadership. On most days it will not be easy; growth never is! But I promise you it will be worth it. I'm confident that this book will help you go to the next level.

After more than five decades of leading, teaching, and mentoring leaders all over the world, I can honestly say that outside of my faith, the decision to grow has impacted my life more than any other. A similar decision lies before you today. So my question for you is simple: What will you do with what you learn from this book? It's not enough to accumulate knowledge without taking action. The people who make a difference in this world intentionally build the bridge between knowing and doing. Will you take the challenge?

To borrow Dianna's beautiful words at the conclusion of this book, "May you continue to become more, as there are countless people eagerly anticipating the full expression of your greatness." I join her as one of those countless people.

Keep climbing, my friend. Because as you become more, we all benefit!

YOUR FRIEND,

John C. Maxwell

A LETTER FROM THE AUTHOR

Dear Reader,

As a leader and a parent, I understand the importance of fostering an environment that encourages people to reach their full potential. Whether you find yourself seated in the boardroom or diligently working around the house, it's inevitable that at certain moments, you'll experience an insatiable yearning for more.

Over the years, there were occasions where I longed for more. Sometimes I wanted more for myself, but I felt this longing acutely when it came to my children or the people I had the privilege and honor to lead. And as I would sit with this longing for more in others, I would often observe these same individuals trapped within their own self-imposed boundaries.

Story after story has been shared with me: some filled with triumph and accomplishments—desires just out of reach—and others riddled with setbacks, wondering how they could ever be successful. Whatever your story, I know it to be immensely significant. Yes, we all have an unchangeable past. Thankfully, the present is malleable and spotless, the cusp of a sky-is-the-limit future. A future I very much hope for you.

This book distills years of research and experience into practical strategies that you can implement immediately. As a visionary leader,

I am confident the Becoming More Model will equip you with the necessary principles, practices, and tools to change your narrative. You are the creator, character, crusader, and champion of your own story.

You can write a better story. A story of intention. A story of achievement. A story of impact. And you can get started on your better story right now.

Within each chapter of this book, you will find invaluable guidance, offering you actionable steps and adjustments to transcend your current circumstance and become more. May you discover and put into practice the principles of moving from limiting to liberating thoughts, beliefs, and mindset; may you harness the four energies of success, cultivate them as integral elements of your daily life, and direct them toward achieving your goals.

It is my sincere desire and intention as you delve into the depths of this book that you view your current circumstances not as obstacles but as springboards catapulting you forward with unwavering enthusiasm. As you embrace the principles and strategies shared, you will not only become more; you will be empowered to accomplish more, acquire more, and ultimately give more. I know firsthand the remarkable growth that people have experienced by committing to follow the model.

Together let's start on your journey to "Becoming More."

WITH MUCH GRATITUDE,
Dianna

Free Companion Material Available

BecomingMoreBook.com/resources
Mindset assessment
Affirmations
Digital copies of models, tables, and more

INTRODUCTION

People are rivers, always ready to move
from one state of being into another.
It is not fair to treat people as if they are finished beings.
Everyone is always becoming and unbecoming.
—KATHLEEN WINTER, *Annabel*

It was one of those pivotal moments that comes along every once in a while. As I sat in a seminar listening to John Maxwell speak, he asked a simple yet intriguing question: "Are you a river or a reservoir? Are you allowing what you learn to flow through you—adding value to others—or are you keeping all you learn to yourself?"

I immediately thought, *I'm a river.* After all, I'm always eager to add value to others, sharing what I know if it will help them. Never can I remember selfishly storing up information.

During a break, a friend and colleague challenged me with a question I wasn't prepared to answer: "Dianna, when are you going to write a book about what you did to go from not being able to afford a babysitter as you started out in real estate to becoming the CEO, growing the largest award-winning coaching company?"

Her question stayed with me long after that seminar was over and haunted me for days and weeks. Even though I had spoken about the power of your mindset for years—helping thousands to transform limiting beliefs into liberating ones—I had never outlined a step-by-step approach from the beginning of my journey for others to review and follow.

My mind began to wander: Was there a connection between the things I had learned and the way I was living? Could I design a clear model for others to follow in the pursuit of becoming more?

I knew that if I did, the model would need to be simple and practical. I began to dream about developing a plan that anyone could put into action. Of course, as things often do, my dream for this book fell to the wayside in favor of other, more pressing tasks. But the need to be a river—to share this model for becoming more with all of you—stayed with me until I couldn't help but begin.

Recognizing that success is a collective effort, I spoke with doctors and accomplished businesspeople, poured myself into research, listened to podcasts, and read numerous books before embarking on a personal mission to create a comprehensive model that can be applied by anyone.

I call the model *Becoming More*.

You may choose to implement this plan on your own, or you might decide to invite your colleagues and friends along on the journey with you. Together, you can engage in discussions about the model, track your personal progress, and mutually support one another along the way.

Regardless of how you approach the model, I'm so thrilled to walk with you as you take the first step toward becoming more. Let's begin!

CHAPTER 1

EMBRACING DIFFERENT

You can't make a difference until you dare to be different.
—ORRIN WOODWARD

D o you want your life to be different? Better? Improved? Maybe you're in a place where you're not certain what you want. One thing I know for sure is that in order to make your life better, you must enter through the gateway of *different*.

> You can't get to better
> until you get to *different*.

Different can be scary. It's uncommon, unfamiliar, and unusual. Yet if you want to become more, entering the realm of different is unavoidable. Becoming more requires you to become better, and becoming better requires you to embrace change. And change happens only through deliberate choice.

Remember Blockbuster? Sears? RadioShack? Do you know what those three companies had in common? They were each once heralded as goliaths in their industries. As the needs of the consumer changed, they chose to remain the same. Did they search for possibilities of becoming more? Did they think about doing something *different*? Did they see choosing *different* as a risk to their current business? We'll never know, yet we can learn from their mistakes.

Your philosophy may be, "If it ain't broke, for heaven's sake, don't break it." Maybe that's a psychological self-protection you've adopted. The status quo might make you feel safe, and it also means you're stuck. Albert Einstein's definition still holds true:

Insanity is doing the same thing over and over again and expecting different results.

Remaining the same and becoming more is an oxymoron—one limits you, while the other liberates you. Opportunities to become more or different exist in your personal as well as your professional life, and though some may seem risky, the greater risk is to remain the same. Sadly, that is the choice too many make, assuming sameness equals stability, when settling for stagnancy can actually cause some to decline into self-sabotage.

You may believe you are the exception. I encourage you to see this in a different light.

The comfort found in sameness can be a risk to each of us. That's because we're more likely to cling to old views and avoid discomfort. And in today's fast-paced, forward-moving world, without progressing, you may think you are standing still—but you're not; you're moving backward. Stand still on a treadmill and you'll be thrown off. (Don't believe me? A quick YouTube search of "treadmill fails" will confirm it.) In the long term, the discomfort you imagine from embracing change will be dwarfed by the discomfort you continue to experience from choosing to hold on to the status quo. The pain of becoming more weighs ounces, while the pain of holding on to the familiar weighs tons.

Are you willing to explore uncharted territories? Think in ways you've never thought? Do what you have never done? Step outside your comfort zone? You *can* if you *will*.

Becoming more doesn't just happen, of course. Like choosing to remain the same, it also begins with a choice. *Choice, change,* and *different* all work together in your quest of becoming more. You'll never *get* your best until you are willing to *give* your best.

YOU FIRST GET TO DIFFERENT THROUGH CHOICE

Has there ever been a time in your life when you made a choice that turned out well, leading you toward success? Did you ever make one that didn't work out so well? Did you learn from it? According to Jean-Paul Sartre, life can be understood as living between points B and D—birth and death. And what comes between those two points? Of course it is C, which represents our choices. Every choice we make shapes our actions, determines our direction, and influences who we ultimately become. Everything in life first originates from a choice.

Creating the life you desire through the power of choice can evoke feelings of intimidation and fear. Feeling forced to make a decision can cause your mind to bounce back and forth, debating and grappling with the best course of action. You may make some choices because you desire to please others. Some people will work diligently to influence or even make the choice for you. Sometimes making decisions entirely by yourself and for yourself can be immensely daunting. Yet even the act of *not* making a choice bears consequences. Do you know what is even more frightening? *Regret.* When you take your final breath, the fears and regrets of others will hold no significance. All that will matter is the choices you made and the life you lived.

With each choice comes *risk,* not knowing precisely where that option will lead. And taking on something new naturally involves experiencing some failures as you go along. Thankfully, these setbacks serve as opportunities to make corrections, ultimately paving the way for future success and growth. As the following diagram shows, you engage in a continuous cycle of learning, implementation, failure, corrections, and learning a new and better way.

ADAPTIVE LEARNING

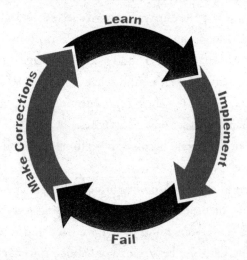

The Adaptive Learning Model © Dianna Kokoszka

Figure 1: The Adaptive Learning Model demonstrates that by engaging in learning, implementation, experiencing failures, and making corrections, you acquire a fresh approach to tackle larger projects, thereby enhancing your cognitive abilities.

You've no doubt heard the saying, "What got you here won't get you there." Your life as you know it, as well as your family and your business, won't rise above who you are *being* at this present moment. Thank goodness *being* is only a temporary state. After all, if we all stayed the same, we would still have to be held or pushed around in a stroller. We are meant to grow: to multiply our talents and *become more*, physically, mentally, and emotionally. I call this the process of *becoming more*.

Following this process means you accept and seize *different*, intentionally working toward becoming more. When I say, "You can become more," do you actually believe me? When I say, "You have greatness inside you," are you inclined to say, "Not me!"? If you are, let me ask you: Did you say that because you feel you should be further along in life than you currently are? If so, you need to know you're not alone. My hope is by the end of this book, your initial response of "Not me!" will transform into "Why not me?"

WHEN CHOICE HITS HOME

Of course, we don't always decide to be different on our own. Sometimes we're forced into it when life deals us a bad hand.

As a teenager, getting ready for school can be uncomfortable and stressful. Doing that alongside—and in competition with—three other siblings and a cousin who lived with us was *more* than stressful for me. It was downright crazy. In an attempt to manage this, my parents gave each of us no more than fifteen minutes in the one and only bathroom every morning. However, the length of time you *actually* got depended very much on where you were in the lineup.

If you were first or second to gain access to the bathroom, life was great. However, when you were fifth—at the end of the line—you were at the mercy of the previous four, some of whom completely lost track of time! Your fifteen minutes could easily shrink to five minutes, and with a fixed 5:30 a.m. departure to Green Valley

Market—the family-owned grocery store where we all worked before school—stress could be at an all-time high.

In an effort to be fair, our parents created a system where they changed the rotation every week, giving everyone their fair share of unfairness.

MY TIME WAS CUT SHORT

On one occasion, I was in the dreaded number five spot, and it was finally my "time" in the bathroom. My brother Larry, at age thirteen, seemed oblivious to this reality, still in the bathroom long after he should have finished. I was patient at first. However, when I had put up with as much of Larry's delinquency as I could stand, I took my rat tail comb, popped the bathroom lock, and pushed open the bathroom door ready to give him a piece of my mind! To my *horror*, I discovered my brother on the floor with a towel around his body and his eyes rolled back, looking very much like he was dead!

You've no doubt heard the phrase "the shot heard 'round the world." Well, I let out a *scream* heard 'round the world— or at least around our neighborhood as Mom, Dad, and other family members came running to see what was happening. From that point on, everything was a blur. My parents jumped into action; Dad called an ambulance while Mom tended to Larry. We all prayed and endured the agonizingly long minutes waiting for help to arrive. Eventually, Mom, Dad, and Larry were in an ambulance racing away from our home in Vernal, Utah, to Salt Lake City, where Larry underwent a number of emergency tests and procedures. After what seemed like forever, we were given the frightening news: Larry had a large tumor at the base of his brain.

Today neuroscience spans a wide range of research, yet this all took place in 1961 when the field of neuroscience was still very much in its infancy. What that meant for Larry and our family was there weren't a lot of treatment options for brain tumors.

And so, with very few "tools" in their toolbox, the hospital staff did the best they could—including surgery. However, after several months, everyone ran out of ideas and there was nothing left to do but send Larry home. There were no real rehab services, so it fell to all of us to do what we could to help Larry "start over" as he was forced to embrace *different*, relearning almost everything, including walking and talking.

Mom and Dad bought a reel-to-reel tape recorder, and for hours after school, when I wasn't working, it was my responsibility and privilege to sit with my brother and teach him how to talk again. The process was painstaking: turning on the reel-to-reel, saying a word, then having Larry say the same word—the best he could—then playing it back, listening for the differences, allowing him to make corrections. This went on for quite some time. Learning, implementing, failing, correcting, and relearning.

Eventually, as Larry advanced, we gave him books to read and record. *The Little Engine That Could*, ironically, was one of those books. And even though, at the time, the main purpose for reading *that* book was to aid Larry's progress in reading and pronunciation, I found myself wondering about the book's simple but profound message. It basically was this: Whether you think you *can*, or you think you *can't*, you're absolutely right. Even at my young age, I wondered about this powerful little phrase: "I think I can." I asked myself over and over, *Does that phrase really work? Does it really make a difference? And if it does, how?*

So, amid juggling my responsibilities at the store, in school, and my involvement with Larry, I managed to carve out moments to visit the library to feed this budding passion of mine—to learn about the human brain and its inner workings. And while I don't think I saw it as clearly at the time, I now see that Larry and I were *testing* the Little Engine's thesis every day (even as my mind was just starting to grapple with its message).

Over time, my brother learned to walk and talk again. Indeed, he did that not just once but four times over the years as he faced numerous other challenges—more brain surgeries, a coma, a stroke, kidney failure, dialysis, and eventually a kidney transplant. The clock kept resetting for Larry, yet each time he chose to fight his way back, to become more with the help of us at first, and then later with his wonderful wife, Vivian, who took on the lion's share of the effort.

As he faced and fought one battle after another, he would often surprise some of the health-care experts, including those who swore he would be in a wheelchair the rest of his life—until the day came that he stood up and walked! Larry never thought about remaining the same. He embraced *different*. Larry's life was altered, yet it never kept him from choosing to become more.

Regrettably, our family's encounters with brain tumors extended beyond Larry's battle. In 1973, my sister Patsy received her own diagnosis. Her tumor was positioned just behind her eye, intertwined with the optical nerve so severely that they could not remove it completely. Over the years, Patsy faced a series of surgeries, hospitalizations, and nursing homes, and—like Larry—bravely fought her battles and kept her positive perspective even as the tumor began to impede her ability to see and articulate the thoughts in her mind. *Different* kept choosing Patsy, and through the differences she relentlessly pursued becoming more. After a stroke, aphasia set in. She knew what she wanted to say, yet the thought would stop midstream, not allowing her to verbally express it. It was challenging for us to guess what she was thinking, so we relied on playing charades, with her acting out her unspoken thoughts. I came to realize how incredibly challenging it must have been for her to know what she wanted to say and not be able to say it quickly, efficiently, and effortlessly. As she struggled to communicate, her words would vanish mid-sentence, followed by a sigh and the words "Ta do, Ta do, Ta do," or "You know." Well, we didn't know, but sometimes we just said we did to move the conversation along.

The tumor would eventually take Patsy's life in her sleep. She, too, was someone from whom I learned many things, especially the importance of not giving up, embracing *different*, leaning into the struggle, and pushing forward as far and as long as you can to always become more. Both Patsy and Larry maintained a fierce determination and demonstrated an unshakable mindset that held firm, even as their bodies gave way before us. They were the living embodiment of the Little Engine That Could: always working to become more than anyone thought they could with an "I think I can" philosophy.

WE CHOOSE TO BECOME BETTER

Larry ignited my curiosity to explore the fundamental components of the brain—the base, the cerebellum, the reticular activating system (RAS), and the unconscious mind. Meanwhile, Patsy lit the fire within me to study how the neocortex and limbic system of the brain work together to allow us to take action and make decisions. I also learned adversity is not an enemy. It is full of teachings such as resourcefulness and resilience, and it presents rewards for those willing to embrace them.

WILL YOU CHOOSE DIFFERENT?

Like Larry and Patsy, your choices will determine everything about your legacy and the story of your life—despite circumstances that might come your way. I have a saying: "When you drink the water, don't forget who dug the well." So my question to you is, Are the choices you make constructing a well that's worth drinking from? Will people talk about the well you dug for them? The ways you empowered them to become better? By embracing *different* and following the teachings in this book, you will have what it takes to be proud of the decisions you make, allowing your legacy to endure through their memories of what you stood for, your principles, your actions, and your generosity.

THE FIRST STEP TO CHANGE

What does your heart truly yearn for? Jot it down, knowing you have the flexibility to edit or expand it later. Awareness is the first step to change. Are you aware of the story you have placed yourself in and who you are currently *being* and *becoming* as a result? If you choose, you can learn how to write a better story.

EMBRACE RESPONSIBILITY

Did you anticipate being where you are today? I've heard it said that 95 percent of the world's population would answer with a resounding *no*. And it's true: We aren't certain where life will take us. Yet we *are* certain that time passes quickly, and things change constantly. Your future will be here before you know it.

The essayist, playwright, and critic George Bernard Shaw wrote, "We are made wise not by the recollection of our past, but by the responsibility for our future." These are sage words to implement into our lives, taking full responsibility for where we are and where we are going. Some people are convinced they are not a member of the "bless me" club, thinking their life is set in stone, taking no responsibility for what happens to them, and always blaming others for their circumstances. My dad always said, "When you point the finger at someone else you have three fingers pointing back at you, so odds are three to one it is your own fault. Embrace responsibility and move on." Taking responsibility for your future drives you to think and do things differently in the present.

We are made wise not by the recollection of our past, but by the responsibility for our future.
—George Bernard Shaw

We live in a time that offers us even fewer certainties, so it should hardly come as a surprise that many people find themselves stressed out. This stress comes from living in conflict with the story that has become their life. Living in a society of constant change means *different* is staring us in the face daily. Forced uncertainty brings doubt, leading to questions such as, "What will happen to me?" and "What will happen to my family?" and "What will happen to my career?"

FRESH THINKING IS REQUIRED

We are already accustomed to fresh thinking. After all, how many of your childhood assumptions have turned out to be false? One false assumption I had early on was thinking I could change others, making them better. What a fallacy that turned out to be! We must first make the choice to change and then spearhead our own advancement. As my mentor for over twenty-five years, John Maxwell, says, "People change when they hurt enough that they have to change, learn enough that they want to change, receive enough that they are able to change."

If you are in your current situation, accepting what you have, beware! You may fall victim to the stories you tell yourself based on past experiences that lock in the belief that life holds no more than you currently have.

AN INVITATION TO BECOME BETTER

At my core, I believe everyone, including you, has a yearning to become more, an incredible potential inside—a vital, living legacy—that is waiting to be lived out. Yet right now you may be anxious, fearful, overwhelmed, unfulfilled, unsupported. It may seem as though a hidden hand is pushing you down and holding you from rising.

Trust me, I know how real that feeling can be. I've been there. And yet *I didn't stay there; neither Larry nor Patsy stayed there; and you don't have to either.* Things do *not* have to be the way they are. Everything can change when you choose to embrace *different* and get on the path to becoming more.

Things I Would Like to Be Different in My Life:
Personal, Business, Relationships, Physical, and Spiritual

CHAPTER 2

GROW WITHIN OR GO WITHOUT

Isn't it odd? We can only see our outsides,
*but nearly **everything** happens on the inside.*
—CHARLIE MACKESY

My son Shane and I were walking along a beach in Mexico when I spotted four sticks strategically placed in the sand with orange netting wrapped around them. The netting was so tight that it reminded me of a shrink-wrapped package that could prevent anyone from even thinking they could break through it. I knew whatever was surrounded by that netting had to be valuable since it was being protected like gold in Fort Knox!

As we got closer, I spotted a sign warning people not to disturb the eggs that were resting on the sandy beach. Shane told me they were turtle eggs, and we should keep an eye on this location as turtle hatchlings usually emerge in masses. If we were around at the right time, we might be able to help the survival rate by keeping would-be predators away as the baby turtles made their way to their new home in the ocean.

Thinking about what I had seen, I reflected on those eggs. I realized that an egg broken by outside forces destroys life within the egg, but an egg broken from the inside brings new life into existence.

You and I are no different from those eggs. Life must be lived from the inside out. Ideas become inventions, dreams become realities, thoughts become actions, intentions become outcomes, the invisible becomes visible, and possibilities become celebrated and cherished memories—or not. Some ideas never amount to anything. Likewise, dreams become frustrations, thoughts remain fantasies, intentions go awry, the invisible never sees the light of day, and possibilities die the slow, soul-destroying death of a thousand excuses.

Do you believe that your external world is more important than your internal world? If so, your brain will always respond to what others think or expect of you. *You must grow within or go without.*

> *When we are no longer able*
> *to change the situation, we are*
> *challenged to change ourselves.*
> —Viktor Frankl

Whether your life is lived well with intention and purpose or lived poorly with disappointment and acquiescence, it is always a function of what is going on within your mind and heart. The quality of our lives is directly influenced by the thoughts, beliefs, values, and truths we hold as well as the practices we adopt, which can either limit us or liberate us. These realities play a pivotal role in determining whether our stories unfold as tragedies or triumphs.

When you have the knowledge and implement it, you can become more, do more, have more, and give more. Note the order I've emphasized here. To do more, have more, and give more, you need to *become* more. People often get this the wrong way around.

It all starts with who you will *be*, not what you have or how hard you work.

BE – DO – HAVE – GIVE

Do you ever feel as if you are going through life simply hoping you are "on the right track" yet feeling as though something is lacking? In nearly every narrative, there exists the characters of victim, villain, and hero. Some stories even feature coaches and mentors.

The person who labels themselves as the victim in their own story believes they must *have* in order to take action and *do*, and only then will they *be*. For example, "If I *have* enough money, then I can *do* what I want and I will *be* successful."

Surprisingly, the villain is the one who thinks the more they *do*, the more they'll *have*, and the more they have, the more successful they will *be*. They believe success is contingent on working longer and harder.

Of course, both victims and villains get the order all wrong. Regardless of whether they believe in HAVE – DO – BE or in DO – HAVE – BE, they often complain about a lack of resources as they resign themselves to the reality they have created. Both unknowingly live their life's story based on the external world, allowing circumstances to dictate who they are.

This is backward to how life actually works.

Frankly, you can be the hero of your own story by realizing life is meant to be lived from the inside out. The hero knows they have to *be* first and that who they are will affect what they *do*. And, in turn, what they *do* will affect what they *have* and what they can ultimately *give*. The hero's philosophy is BE – DO – HAVE – GIVE.

The great part of your life's story is that you can change from victim or villain to hero. You no longer have to accept the circumstances you find yourself in. And when you hit a rough patch on your journey, remember you can get your life in order by thinking about who you need to *be*. (Not what you can have or how hard you can work.) It is about who you are. George Bernard Shaw observed, "The reasonable man adapts himself to the world. The unreasonable man adapts the world to himself."

Are you ready to follow that advice? If so, then embrace the new thoughts and hopes of change that are already whirling through your mind. Like the fruit that is ready to harvest, you are ripe with potential. Be honest with yourself. Dig deep into those forgotten places of your heart and open yourself up to the possibility of greatness. Realize that who you are at this moment isn't set in stone. By learning new things and implementing them, you will chip away at who you are, becoming more than you ever thought possible.

SHAPING THE STONE

In 1464, Agostino di Duccio began sculpting an exceptionally large block of marble but gave up. Along came Antonio Rossellino in 1475, and he thought he would work at sculpting it. Eventually, he, too, abandoned the project. Both men walked away saying there were too many *taroli* (imperfections) that would threaten the stability of the statue.

This marble block sat neglected for more than twenty-five years, untouched, until 1501, when a young artist, Michelangelo, only twenty-six years of age, came along, looked at the slab, and saw something different than his predecessors. His words have been preserved for posterity: "Every block of stone has a statue inside it, and it is the task of the sculptor to discover it. I saw the angel in the marble and carved it until I set him free."[1]

He saw a beautiful figure "trapped" in a flawed block of marble. As a sculptor, his task was to chip away at the unwanted marble until he freed the hero inside. He envisioned taking it from being a block of deficient marble to a masterpiece of human form and beauty. Because of his ability to see what was invisible, we can all now appreciate the statue *David*.

Can you imagine yourself as a modern-day Michelangelo and your life as a piece of marble that takes the form of the flawed stories you've been telling yourself? No matter how imperfect or flawed your background or situations might have been, you are the sculptor, capable of setting your inner hero free. You have the power to chip away at all of your limiting thoughts, beliefs, values, emotions, and language so that a new story emerges. Let yourself be developed from the inside out.

Releasing your greatness and possibilities is an *inside* job that will reveal itself to the *outside* world.

CHANGE YOUR MIND

Dr. Dharius Daniels says, "You don't change your life by changing your life. You change your life by changing your mind." In other words:

When you open your mind to new ideas, you start on a path to better.

And when you get better, your life gets better.

When you get better, your family gets better.

---

[1] "How a Rejected Block of Marble Became the World's Most Famous Statue," *Encyclopaedia Britannica*, https://www.britannica.com/story/how-a-rejected-block-of-marble-became-the-worlds-most-famous-statue; Joanne M. Anderson, "All About the Art and Science of Stone Carving," *Masonry*, https://www.masonrymagazine.com/blog/2018/03/29/all-about-the-art-and-science-of-stone-carving/.

When you get better, your business gets better.

When you get better, you can even change the world!

It all begins in your mind. Every aspect of your life grows to the extent that you do. Break out of who you are being and become more than you are now. Release the bonds that limit you and free yourself to improve your relationships, your business, and your life story from this chapter forward.

It takes only one person to change your life—and that's you.

Are you ready?

Read on.

Who Would You Like to BE?

_____

_____

_____

What Would You Like to DO?

_____

_____

_____

What Would You Like to HAVE?

_____

_____

_____

What Would You Like to GIVE and to Whom?

_____

_____

_____

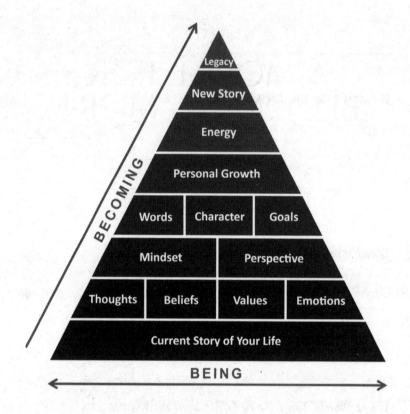

Becoming More Model © Dianna Kokoszka

Figure 2: The Becoming More Model encompasses every facet of your life that you will actively develop to continuously evolve and progress. It is a model that you will repeatedly navigate, focusing on one aspect at a time, transitioning from your present narrative to a new one, ultimately shaping your legacy.

CHAPTER 3

A MODEL FOR BECOMING MORE

The Amazon, the greatest river on Earth, is a powerful teacher.
It reminds us to flow with grace, adapt to change,
and carve our own path through the obstacles.
—PAULO COELHO

We've talked a lot about *why* you should get started on this journey. And in this chapter, we're going to discuss *how* you'll make it happen. Let's begin by taking a look at the Becoming More Model.

This pyramid represents the process of becoming more, starting in the present with who you are now—the Current Story of Your Life—and moving you *up* toward your New Story, the life that will become your Legacy.

As this book unfolds, we will look at each component of the pyramid in detail. To start, let's get acquainted with each block and see how they build on one another.

Your thought life influences everything that follows. Thoughts encircle your mind and develop into Beliefs that you accept as truth. Beliefs serve as nutrition for your Values, which anchor and guide your life. All three of these components drive and respond to your Emotions.

These four characteristics work together to make up your Mindset and lead to your Perspective—how you think about and view the world.

You may never have thought you could control these parts of your personality. The good news is—you absolutely can! So let's keep climbing the pyramid.

Your Mindset and Perspective then transform your choice of Words, your Character, and your Goals. By following the Becoming More Model, you'll discover renewed ambition and enthusiasm in this level of the pyramid as you move toward continuous personal growth. Before you know it, you will find the Energy of confidence, optimism, purpose, and gratitude displaying ample proof that you are indeed rewriting your old story and watching it become your New Story, ultimately forming your Legacy.

BECOMING MIGHTY STARTS SMALL

Of course, progressing through the levels of the pyramid won't happen instantly. Change takes time; forming habits requires consistency. Greatness is more like a Crock-Pot than a microwave.

One day in July 2021, I was flying home from Brazil after an event for EQUIP, a nonprofit organization. I was looking out the window and saw a magnificent river. I found myself thinking of the continent's great Amazon River and how it was uniquely formed. Not believing in coincidences, I wasn't surprised when later that week, my sister Raelene shared a video with me about the river.

It showed how the Solimões River starts high in the Andes Mountains of South America, where melting snow gathers to form a great river that grows in size and strength as it winds down the mountains to the Brazilian valley. Along the way, it collects soil from the mountains and canyons and carries them along with it, making the river cloudy brown in color. It courses through the lowlands of the Amazon jungle for nearly a thousand miles, carving out its own path.

To the north, the lush green jungles of Brazil give birth to another mighty river, the Rio Negro. This river also picks up minerals and elements from the jungle floor, transforming its waters to a clear yet mysterious dark current. For 1,400 miles, the Rio Negro travels much like its cousin the Solimões—that is to say, in splendid isolation, gaining strength on its journey, yet independent of the other. Then something powerful happens. The fast, sediment-filled currents of the Solimões collide with the slower and clearer current of the Rio Negro near the warm jungles of northern Brazil. For a while, despite having collided, the two great rivers flow side by side, unmixed, for many miles, with the Solimões looking brown and dirty and the Rio Negro clear. The distinction is so dramatic it looks as if someone drew a line in the river, each preserving its distinctive properties and appearances—as if to say, "I am so mighty you will not change me!"

Astonishingly, the ground beneath the waters declines and the two rivers begin to flow faster, churning and mixing with each other. Eventually they blend completely to form one of the strongest rivers in the world: the Amazon.

Consider the pyramid model once again. Perhaps you think the various blocks in the triangle are different, each unique, coursing through life alone, representing solitary concerns. But in truth, they all merge and flow together. With this in mind you may be asking yourself, *How can I possibly flow them all together as one, becoming more than I am? How can I unite all the independent models and components given in this book to write a new story of my life, becoming more successful and more significant, eventually leaving a legacy?*

Picture of the confluence point. Where the two rivers meet you observe a clear distinction between the contrasting colors and textures of the water. One is clear, the other is murky, creating a visible boundary. ©rovsky via canva.com

Like these two magnificent, independent rivers, each segment of the model flows together. It may happen deep in the currents of your subconscious mind where you are not aware. Trust me, it will happen as surely as the Solimões and Rio Negro form the Amazon if you will simply commit to moving up the pyramid with confidence.

Here is one last thought to remember as you begin working toward being the hero of your own story:

We are imperfect people living
in an imperfect world,
and when it comes to people
that is the only perfect truth.

Be intentional with your work, not judgmental with yourself as you work through the model. If the answer is no, then that's OK. Your journey is about to take a wondrous turn. Embrace it with all your passion.

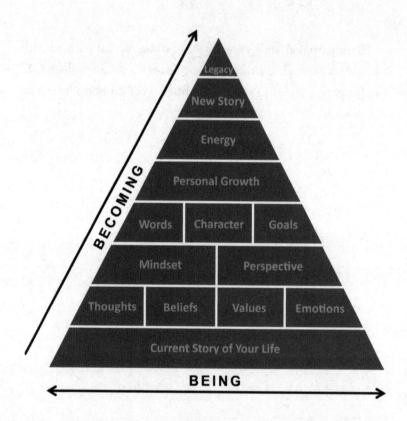

CHAPTER 4

FROM HUMAN BEING TO HUMAN BECOMING

How do you become a butterfly? You stop being a caterpillar.
—Adapted from Trina Paulus, *Hope for the Flowers*

Similar to a butterfly's metamorphosis, which takes it from crawling on the ground to soaring through the air, you can embark on a path of transformation. Becoming more is a two-stage process that requires both deconstruction and reconstruction. It starts with who you are right now, discovering and tearing down what limits you (deconstruction), and then recreating your life in the direction of becoming more (reconstruction).

Take a moment to contemplate your current position. I venture to say that there exists a gap between where you are and where you desire to be. However, I firmly believe that you possess a distinctive capability, a gift that sets you apart. Think about what that might be, for it will help fill the gap.

Working in the grocery store at the age of five didn't offer many tasks I could perform at a high level. Mom and Dad, in their wisdom, made me manager of the magazine rack: my own domain to control and make certain all the magazines were stocked and looking great. Desiring to sell as many magazines as I could to impress my parents, I listened when Dad taught me that if someone picked up a car magazine, I was to quickly point out all the other magazines that had cars on the front and say, "If you like that one, you'll want to buy these too." When I advanced to being a checker at the register, I was instructed that if someone was buying ice cream to ask them if they would like chocolate or caramel toppings, whipped cream, or root beer for floats. There was always something you could add. Maybe that's why I truly believe you can always become more, adding and multiplying to who you are being today. Maybe you think it's too late, you are too old, or luck has passed you by. If so, consider Tom Brady, one of the most celebrated football players in history. He led his teams to win a record number of Super Bowls and was named Most Valuable Player (MVP) five times. The NFL recognized him three times as the MVP. His career is legendary. Did you know that, up until ninth grade, he wasn't even interested in football?

Knowing other boys began learning the sport around third grade didn't stop him. As a high school sophomore, he was offered an opportunity to play when the first-string quarterback quit. The following year, he earned the position of starting quarterback. In college, Brady found there were seven other quarterbacks vying for the same position. Thinking he didn't stand a chance, he considered transferring yet stuck it out. As he worked diligently to become better, it wasn't until his junior year that he eventually rose to first-string quarterback.

His desire to play in the NFL continued to grow, bringing on yet another challenge to face. No one seemed interested in him. It wasn't until the sixth round of the 2000 draft, on the 199th pick, that he was finally chosen by the New England Patriots.

Brady didn't have the best stats or the physical structure that the pros were looking for. What he did have was grit. His determination to grow from who he was *being* to *becoming more* was unmatched. As of 2022, Brady had won the most championships by any one player and the most games by any quarterback, led the most fourth-quarter comebacks, and the list goes on. The players selected Brady, at age forty-five, as the number one player for the 2022 season. He is someone who realizes you never rest at being; it is always about *becoming more.*

Do you think you can become the most valuable player in your life? Do you really believe in the possibility of more? Take encouragement from another sports legend, Muhammad Ali, who reminded us, "Impossible is just a big word thrown around by small men who find it easier to live in the world they've been given than to explore the power they have to change it." Impossible is not a fact. It's an opinion. Impossible is pent-up potential. Impossible is temporary. Impossible is nothing.

Change Impossible to I'm Possible

YOUR OWN STORY

From the moment we're born, we arrive amid a story already in progress. We don't recognize this when we're very young; however, we learn soon enough as the pieces fall into place. You might be tempted to believe the story you were born into limits you from moving beyond your current circumstances. But does it?

How many people do you know who seem to be completely different from their siblings, despite growing up in the same environment? There is an old tale of two boys who grew up in a home where the parents were alcoholics. They ended up living very different lives.

One was very successful and the other landed up on the streets. When they were asked why they felt their life had gone the way it had, they answered the same way: "I am this way because my parents were alcoholics."

Was it their DNA? Their nature? Their nurturing? Or was it strictly a choice?

NATURE AND NURTURE

Our DNA, our *nature*, refers to our hereditary factors and genetic profile. *Nurture* refers to our environments, culture, friends, the experiences we are exposed to, and how they impact us. Everything we are subjected to helps shape us.

As we look at how nurturing affects who we become, information published by the British Psychological Society reveals an interesting pattern based on children brought up in homes where judgment runs rampant. In this environment, children are judged based on a merit system. The parents' interpretation of the child's actions determines whether the child gets scolded or praised.

It doesn't take much scolding before the child feels fearful with a high level of anxiety. Desiring to please the parents and avoid the torment of the screaming and sometimes physical abuse that follows creates more anxiety. To avoid the pain, the child does nearly anything to please the parent. Their nervous system has been conditioned to see a risk of failure as a surefire way to disappoint their parents, causing a neurological response equivalent to life or death.

When there are high doses of fear or failure in the home, the child tends to have no motivation for school. Of course, survival requires them to obtain good grades, not for personal or affirming reasons but to appease their parents. The study went on to say that this environment perpetuates the same pattern in the next generation as well as for generations to come.[1]

So it makes sense that you might feel stuck in the patterns of your parents and their parents and their parents. It also means that the choices you make today will not only affect you but also shape future generations. In fact, research shows that your decisions make changes to your DNA that will be passed down to your lineage.

Thankfully, as the author of your own story, you have the ability to break free from the patterns of your ancestors and to chart a new path for your descendants. But it won't be easy.

A WHOLE VILLAGE CHANGES

In his January 2010 *TIME* magazine article "Why Genes Aren't Destiny," writer and journalist John Cloud unearthed the fascinating story of the small, nineteenth-century municipality of Överkalix in Sweden. Living in an isolated area with a tiny population subject to a harsh climate, the inhabitants grew everything they ate.

When bad harvests came, and they were frequent, many would starve. However, there were also intermittent seasons of extreme abundance during which the people would overeat and binge. Wondering what long-term effects this unpredictable feast-and-famine lifestyle had on the children growing up in the region, Dr. Lars Olov Bygren made an intriguing discovery: the boys who went from normal eating to gluttony in a single season lived shorter lives and produced children who lived shorter lives by six years. Even more, their grandsons lived six years less than the grandsons of those who endured the poor harvests and didn't overeat.

In calculating certain socioeconomic variations, Bygren, his team of researchers, and others studying this unique case found that

---

[1] Adelphi Psych Medicine Clinic, https://adelphipsych.sg/author/joeihuang.

drops in lifetime longevity applied in females as well. This was all true even after they moved out of the area!

"To put it simply, the data suggested that a single winter of overeating as a youngster could initiate a biological chain of events that would lead one's children, grandchildren and their children to pass decades earlier than their peers did."[2]

The results were seen over generations! Why would this happen? The answer lies in the field of epigenetics. Although a new science, it is now known that the actions you take continuously—habits—attach to a chain that has been building from the beginning of time, with traits and behaviors passing from your ancestors to you, from you to your children, and from them to their children for generations to come.[3]

This shows us how we are influenced by past generations and how we influence future generations, in a very direct, biological way—more than we realize. Many of us have read the stories of how twins with the same DNA, adopted or separated from birth, can inherit the same mannerisms and similar interests. In some cases, twin boys married women with the same name![4] But epigenetics tells us even more.

We all have billions of cells and are each born with a genetic code or blueprint that receives signals from our own environment. These signals activate and silence different genes that impact how much, or how little, certain parts of our code will be expressed. Modifications to our DNA are called our epigenome (hence,

---

[2] Lars Olov Bygren, cited in John Cloud, "Why Genes Aren't Destiny," *TIME*, January 6, 2010, https://content.time.com/time/subscriber/article/0,33009,1952313,00.html.

[3] "A Super Brief and Basic Explanation of Epigenetics for Total Beginners," WhatIsEpigenetics, September 1, 2019, https://www.whatisepigenetics.com/what-is-epigenetics/.

[4] Edwin Chen, "Twins Reared Apart: A Living Lab," *New York Times*, December 9, 1979, https://www.nytimes.com/1979/12/09/archives/twins-reared-apart-a-living-lab.html.

epigenetics). Exposure to toxins, physical exercise, or stress all affect the epigenome, making each of us unique. The code therefore changes based on what we do, what we eat, who we hang out with, what we learn, and our experiences. Let me emphasize *who we hang out with*, for it has been said (and now there is proof) that you become like your closest friends.

> *Be careful of the environment*
> *you choose for it will shape you.*
> *Be careful of the friends you choose*
> *for you will become like them.*
> —W. CLEMENT STONE

This genetic malleability through our environment and choices could explain why many other identical twins who have the same DNA and grew up in the same household show significant differences when they're older, as evidenced by their skills, their achievements, their health, and their overall outlook in life.[5]

Remarkably, epigenetics shows us how we can play an active role in shaping ourselves into the people we desire to become. It's the bridge between *nature* and *nurture*. The idea that our genes are set in stone—that they determine everything—is simply not true. Neither is it true that we're mere products of our environment. *Our choices matter.* Like the siblings who ended up on opposing sides of the success spectrum, both crediting their alcoholic parents, the past does not define who a person becomes. "It's not what's in your past, and it's not even what's in your future, they both pale in comparison to what is inside of you

---

5 Sarah Graham, "Identical Twins Exhibit Differences in Gene Expression," *Scientific American*, July 5, 2005, accessed July 2022, https://www.scientificamerican.com/article/identical-twins-exhibit-d/.

and the choices you make today."[6] When it comes to whether nature or nurture contributes more to our personality, it's like asking which contributes more to the area of a rectangle, its length or its width? Both are important—and what's more, both can be changed!

Here's the best part! As a human being, you are not *fixed*. You are free, much freer than you realize, to become more—much more than you currently are. You were born as a daughter, sister, son, brother, niece, or nephew, and as time passes, you might become a mother, father, aunt, uncle, grandmother, grandfather, colleague, boss, and a million other things. You wear multiple hats that define your various forms of being—in other words, your *roles*. And these roles go beyond your first connections such as family and extended family into the ever-widening world that encompasses your employment, your civic involvement, your leisurely pursuits, and your circle of friends.

DON'T GET CAUGHT IN THE GAP TRAP

All the different roles you take on shape and mold you in a never-ending process where you are simultaneously being who you are and becoming who you are not yet. The challenge, however, comes when amid the demands of day-to-day life you lose sight of the *becoming* side of your life, expressed by the gap widening between who you are and who you desire to be.

Your days may be full of events and your schedule might be brimming with activities. You may feel, and even believe, that you're going somewhere and becoming somebody you desire to be. But without a passion, a goal, and a plan, you're just, well, going.

Are you living in the moment or are you stuck in the moment, always busying yourself with updating your to-do or to-have list? Do

[6] Kevin Mitchell, "Epigenetics: What Impact Does It Have on Our Psychology?" Trinity College Dublin, January 28, 2019, https://www.tcd.ie/news_events/articles /epigenetics-what-impact-does-it-have-on-our-psychology/.

you have a to-be list or, better yet, a *to-become* list? I would submit that these latter lists are more important. Creating your to-become list will help you prioritize your to-have and to-do lists because you will be more aware of what is truly important.

Go ahead and start writing your to-become list now. Come back to it tomorrow and keep expanding on it, making it clearer. Clarity will give you power, and over time you will find yourself beginning to understand who you truly desire to become.

BECOMING, NOT JUST BEING

What if you focus on calling yourself a human *becoming*, willing to embrace the reality that you are *unfinished* business? Remember, who you will become, you are becoming right now.

How much greater might your impact be if the shotgun pattern of your countless activities was tightened into the coordinated and concentrated force of a single bullet as it powers to, and beyond, the target—beyond just what you need to do or want to have, expanding to who you are becoming?

You may be living in the past and hanging on to one great accomplishment. Even so, your past accomplishments aren't going to get you on a stained-glass window anytime soon. Or you may find yourself in a rut and intend to climb out. Either way, you need to see yourself simultaneously from two perspectives: understanding who you have been up to this point and committing to becoming more.

While there is no value in living in the past, there is great value in learning from the past, as long as you do so with purpose. Reflection that does not result in renovation is without value.

Contrary to popular belief, experience by itself is not automatically a great teacher. We all know people who have plenty of experiences and who have, nevertheless, not learned a great deal from them. Why? Because it's only when we *reflect* on our experiences, *evaluate* them, and *use this evaluation as the basis for change* that these experiences can truly be called one of our greatest teachers.

Once I was told of a high school that was looking to fill a job vacancy when its longtime principal announced his retirement. A search committee narrowed the candidates to two individuals, one who had been at the school for eight years and another who had been there for twenty years. The position ultimately went to the teacher who had been there eight years. When the other candidate discovered he was not chosen, he aired his complaints with the search committee, pointing out he had far more experience than the selected candidate. In response, the committee gently informed him that although he had spent twenty years at the school, he did not in fact have twenty years of experience. In the committee's view, it was more accurate to say he had accumulated closer to four years of experience and then repeated those four years five times.

What happened? He succumbed to complacency and lived in his comfort zone, something that threatens all of us when we cease to make growth a conscious and deliberate activity. Experience, if not reflected on and evaluated, isn't all it's cracked up to be. The key is to always work to be your best in the present while also working to become better for the future. The ceiling you have made for yourself today must be the floor you stand on tomorrow. That's why, in light of our past, we don't just stay there—rather, we commit to *becoming more*.

COMMIT TO THE PROCESS OF CHANGE

One way of thinking about *becoming* was captured by Jeff Henderson, an entrepreneur, pastor, and author of the wonderful book *Know What You're FOR: A Growth Strategy for Work, an Even Better Strategy for Life.*[7] He asks the important question, "Does what you want to be known for match what you *are* known for?" What I admire is that Henderson points to yet another gap trap between who we think we are and who others think we are. By simply making a commitment to become more, providence moves you toward a place where the perception of you by others more closely matches the reality of the life you live.

This process is far from ambiguous or obscure. In fact, I have meticulously mapped it out for you in the comprehensive model.

When I am speaking of a commitment to change, I'm talking about the active verb *to change*: a conscious, intentional act of will that starts from within—within your relationships, your thoughts, beliefs, values, and emotions—and is expressed in your choices and behaviors. All these become habits that change the world, leaving behind powerful legacies. This is what you will be known for when you have made your final contribution to the world. It may be a small contribution or a large one. What matters most is that it will be yours and it will come about intentionally.

In the docuseries *The Last Dance*, basketball legend Michael Jordan detailed how he intentionally, repeatedly pushed himself to become better than he was in his previous game. You don't have to be the greatest of all time at what you do, yet if you work to be 1 percent better every day, you will be amazed at who you become.

READY TO BREAK FREE?

You deserve to soar. Like a butterfly, you will go through disruption, maybe even struggle, confusion, and breakdowns, entering your own metamorphosis. Embrace tomorrow with enthusiasm, for after a

---

[7] Jeff Henderson, *Know What You're FOR: A Growth Strategy for Work, an Even Better Strategy for Life* (Grand Rapids, MI: Zondervan, 2019).

breakdown comes a breakthrough—leaving behind your cocoon.

On the other side is a gift—an older, wiser, more passionate, more savvy, more daring, and more accomplished version of yourself, of the person you were made to be.

You have a gift beautifully wrapped. The question is . . . will you open it?

I will show you how.

My To-Become List

_____

_____

_____

_____

_____

_____

_____

_____

_____

I Am Making a Commitment to Myself to Become More

_____

_____

_____

_____

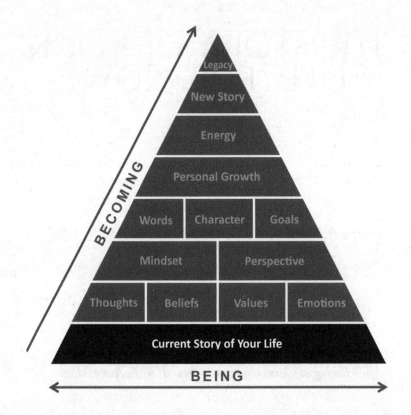

CHAPTER 5

THE STORY OF YOUR LIFE (FOR NOW)

We are, as a species, addicted to stories.
Even when the body goes to sleep,
the mind stays up all night, telling itself stories.
—JONATHAN GOTTSCHALL

As kids we loved playing outside, running all over the open fields until we heard our parents persistently calling out to us with the same words every night. It was just four words. Four words that my siblings and I hated to hear:

"It's time for bed!"

They fell so easily from my parents' lips but landed hard on our youthful ears, always coming too early in the evening—and never welcome! On the surface, the words had the *appearance* of a mere announcement, yet underneath there was an implied command with consequences for resisting.

But sometimes the initial four words were followed by four additional words that turned the dreaded announcement into a delightful invitation:

"Let's read a story!"

Those words changed everything, at least for me, because it meant my mother or grandmother would soon be tapping into our imaginations and taking us to far-off places—without ever leaving the room!

One evening when I was about eight years old, Grandma read to us from Charles Dickens's *David Copperfield* and, like many kids, I put myself into the book as one of the characters. When she came to the part where David Copperfield says, "Whether I shall turn out to be the hero of my own life, or whether that station will be held by anybody else, these pages must show," I remember being quite captivated. That word *hero* intrigued me and threw me into a bit of a quandary. Up until that point, the only heroes I knew of were from comic books in which the main character was the hero for somebody else. Copperfield's statement read differently and made me wonder how anyone could be the hero of their *own* story.

The comic book world at the time was dominated by men— Superman, Batman, Captain America—with the only mainstream exception being Wonder Woman. We shared the same first name, and I felt an absolute connection with her. I would often imagine what it might be like to be her. *No* damsel in distress for me. I wanted to dominate and triumph as a leader, like Wonder Woman. I wanted to have her lasso of truth, her integrity, her super speed, and to be driven by the power of love and equality for all people.

Of course, at that early age I had no concept that I held the pen and, with the choices I made, could write my own story. I don't recall anyone ever asking, or even gently nudging me, to design my life. No one told me that if I didn't intentionally create my own story, I would automatically fade into the storyline of others. But the seed was planted nonetheless.

How about you? Did anyone ever tell you that you were

responsible to write your own story? Have you ever thought about what makes you unique? Are you allowing your gifts to show up in the stories you tell and act out? Sometimes our stories are so well ingrained and rehearsed that they become a habitual way of life.

> *The chains of habit are*
> *too light to be felt until*
> *they are too strong to be broken.*
> —WARREN BUFFETT

Will you live a story that you design or one that you accept by default? If you don't create your own life story, chances are you will fall into someone else's. And guess what kind of story they may have planned for you? One that serves them!

STORIES LIMIT OR LIBERATE US

Stories are the foundation we build our lives on. They transfer information, connect events, transcend generations, and are always evolving. Each story has a plot, conflict, resolution, theme, symbolism, point of view, and perspective. In chapter 2 we talked about the characters a story contains and the categories they fall into, including the Victim you feel sympathy for, the Villain you dislike, the Hero you cheer for, and the Coach and/or Mentor you respect. These characters exist in stories not only because they exist in the real world but also because they exist inside our heads.

Those who play the Victim tell stories where someone has wronged them.

The role of the Villain concentrates on telling stories when they overpowered someone.

The Hero tells stories of overcoming challenges, achieving success, and growth.

The Coach's stories are of advancement, production, and breakthroughs to expand thinking.

The Mentor shares stories of their wisdom gained in their personal life as well as their career to illuminate different perspectives, thus providing a new experience for the mentee.

To be intentional about creating your own story, you must decide which character you will play. Will you be the victim or villain—limiting your journey? Or will you choose to be the hero, a coach, or a mentor, walking in liberation?

Limiting and Liberating Characters

Characters We Choose to Play				
Limiting			Liberating	
Victim	Villain	Hero	Coach	Mentor
The target	Brute	Overcomer	Motivator	Teacher
Whipping post	Bully	Achiever	Challenger	Adviser
Fall guy	Scoundrel	Rescuer	Strategist	Empowerer
Prey	Snake	Warrior	Equipper	Guide
Laughingstock	Cutthroat	Champion	Maximizer	Shepherd

Which role(s) have you played in the past? Which will you intentionally play in the future? Throughout my life I have played many of these roles. While others may have cast me into a part, ultimately, I am the one who chose to accept it—or reject it.

We must realize that it's not up to someone else to liberate us. We must choose to liberate ourselves. This starts by choosing the part we will play in the story of our life.

THE CHOICE IS UP TO YOU

If anybody should get a pass for taking on the role of victim, it would be Yisrael Kristal.

In the book *Morality: Restoring the Common Good in Divided Times*, the late British author and statesman Jonathan Sacks told the story of Kristal, who passed away on August 11, 2017, just short of his 114th birthday. But Sacks wasn't interested in celebrating Kristal's distinction as one of the world's ten longest-lived people. He was interested in Kristal's ability to triumph in the face of adversity. To me his story was about going from victim to mentor *through choice*.

You see, Kristal was a Holocaust survivor. He survived four years in the Lodz Ghetto and was later transported to the death camp of Auschwitz. His two children died in Lodz, and his wife was killed in Auschwitz. When he was liberated, he weighed eighty-two pounds and was the only member of his extended family to have survived. Despite the horror that had befallen him, he refused to withdraw. Kristal chose to tell his story about the experience, affirming his commitment never to yield to victimhood.

After all, he had suffered a great deal during one of the worst crimes against humanity in all of history. Not only did he refuse to play the role of victim he also chose not to be cast as a villain working at retaliating against his oppressors. Instead, he chose to look ahead, as David Sacks said, "with almost superhuman, hero courage" to build a new life for himself. Kristal realized he had to create his own story—to be the main character as well as the crusader and champion of his own life. He chose to be the hero for himself and a mentor for others.

The point of my retelling this is not to shame you into acknowledging that you don't have it so bad compared to Holocaust survivors.

I believe that most people suffer, some considerably more than others. And we all fall, from time to time, into a major rut that saps our motivation to become more. No, my purpose here is to shine light on Mr. Kristal's epic resilience and to show you a stark example of the "pastness" of the past. Remember, your past is exactly that— your past. You cannot change it; you can only respond to it. Change can happen only in the present moment; therefore, the changes you make today will determine the stories of your tomorrow.

Kristal's life, your life, my life is not just about us. Our stories cocreate and intersect with others'. Indeed, I have come to see that "story" is an inescapable reality for everyone on the planet. There are no "story-free" people. All of us are living out our stories—every hour of every single day. What stories are you living out? What stories are you *speaking* and *sharing* with the world? Some might be long or short, simple or complex—whatever it is, it's a story, and it's *yours*. And your story influences the stories of others.

HOME IS WHERE YOUR STORY BEGINS

From the moment we take our first breath of life, we step into a narrative already in progress. Perhaps you were a star from day one, welcomed with open arms by parents who celebrated your every move and sound. Or maybe they were forced to let you in, reluctantly casting you as an extra or in a supporting role to themselves or your siblings, where their story took precedence over yours.

During childhood, the stories we encounter—from our parents, relatives, teachers, and the broader culture—guide us, unveiling the truths of life and imparting lessons for our journey ahead. Stories teach us how to navigate relationships, comprehend our past, and make sense of the world around us. The tapestry of our lives is woven by the stories we are told. These stories created the very fabric of our being. It tells others the essentials about the where, what, why, and how of our life.

YOUR LIFE STORY

Your stories come from your inner world, making up a book of life with your name on it. Stop and think for a moment; how have you been living up to this point? Is it a captivating book? How does it read? Is it an adventure, a romance, mystery, tragedy, all about business, or a fairy tale? The way you describe your story eventually becomes your autobiography. Stories are the glue that binds your life experiences and forms who you become.

Few people realize the full extent to which they are the creator, main character, crusader, and champion of their own life story. They usually chalk their story up to fate or a throw of the dice, which is unsatisfactory because fate is a terrible creator of stories. You may say God is writing your story, yet he has given you agency, which means in a way you hold the pen to cocreate through choice. This offers endless possibilities when you embrace the idea that you are responsible for how your story will read. It doesn't matter what your life has been thus far; what matters is where it is going and how it will end. After all, the wake of a boat doesn't drive it any more than your past drives your future. Think bigger and be open to a new reality.

STORIES REVEAL OUR HEART

The stories you tell ultimately reveal your heart, exposing who you are, where you are going, and what is important to you. What stories are you known for? When you change the way you tell your story, you change the way the world responds to you.

If I am interviewing you for a position at my company and ask you to tell me a story about yourself, the story and the way you tell it will reveal if you will come into my employment as a victim who is always going to be whining instead of winning, a villain who will likely pounce on anybody who gets in your way, or a hero with a desire to add value to others.

STORIES ARE TOLD BECAUSE WE WANT SOMETHING

Some tell stories to gain empathy, while others tell stories to brag on their accomplishments. Each story is based on our experience and what we desire to portray as an outcome.

Knowing the power of stories, why not ask others to share their stories so you get to know them better? You will find a profound connection between value and story, as the truths are often wrapped within the fabric of a narrative. Life itself makes storytelling a compelling and predictive force on the journey to becoming more. The sheer circumstances you find yourself in compel you to create a story. Why do you do this? Well, as Aristotle once said, "Nature abhors a vacuum," and so do our brains. The brain hypothesizes possible explanations and pieces together a pattern. In other words, it begins to write a story that *explains* the puzzling circumstances.

STORIES ARE CREATED TO SURVIVE

The brain is often likened to a computer, yet when you type words on a computer you can read them back the same way time and time again. Your brain, on the other hand, cannot reiterate a story exactly word for word. What it *does* do is store memories from your experiences. Your reactive brain then tells and retells a story, sometimes embellishing portions, leaving parts out—or worse yet, making up details to fit the situation you find yourself in. What began as a single experience grows into an explanation for many related or unrelated experiences. When people tell stories over and over again, even if they are bald-faced lies—false as a fairy tale—they are etching them into their brain like a tattoo, believing them to the point they would testify on a witness stand that they are true.

How does it all work? The following diagram and accompanying explanations give us an overview of how our brains take in experiences and form a story. You have the ability to train your brain to stop the cycle by only creating stories you wish to accept.

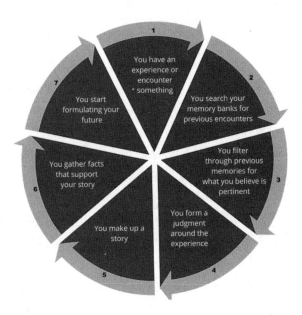

Story Formation Model © Dianna Kokoszka

Figure 3: The Story Formation Model illustrates the process of crafting narratives and highlights that altering our internal storytelling shapes the range of information we gather to support our future.

1. As you go throughout your day, you have many experiences.

2. For each event, your brain shuffles through the maps you have

built in your memory banks, much like searching through a filing cabinet or photo album, for previous encounters of the same type of experience.

3. Filtering through your previous memories, you select what is pertinent.

4. You make a judgment within the blink of an eye. (Your brain is a judging machine, always comparing.)

5. Once you form a judgment, you make up a story based on your interpretation of what is happening. Your brain does not care if your interpretation is true.

6. Desiring to look good and be right, you gather evidence to support your newly formed story, filtering out all information and possibilities that do not reinforce your new beliefs. The reticular activating system, a network of neurons located in the brain stem, is like your own Google search engine, built in your head. You tell it what to look for and it goes to work filtering through all available distractions, allowing you to see only what you believe to be true or important.

7. Now, with all other possibilities eliminated, you give direction to your future.

The eyes only see and
the ears only hear what
the brain is looking for.
—DAN SULLIVAN

However, what if an event occurs and your interpretation is not right? What if you are missing key information, or your experience doesn't give you enough choices to place what happened in a larger, more understandable framework? What if you have come to a conclusion too quickly? This is why we should not be quick to judge but more open to *growth*, asking questions and listening to help formulate our story.

CHANGE YOUR STORY, CHANGE YOUR LIFE

You may be thinking it really doesn't matter how you tell your story to yourself or others. These narratives exist whether you choose to acknowledge them or not, right? Research shows that the way you think and the way you tell your story have profound effects on the kind of person you become.

Dan P. McAdams of Northwestern University expounded on this in his seminal paper, "The Psychology of Life Stories."

In one study, volunteers wrote narratives featuring redemptive sequences, where a failure changed them for the better. The researchers then compared these narratives with participants who weren't prompted to include redemption in their accounts. Those encouraged to tell stories of redemptive experiences showed a greater goal persistence, tending to finish what they started.

Not only did these findings provide evidence that personal narratives can be shaped, the researchers also concluded that shifting the way people think and tell their stories around important events can influence their lives in the future. That is the purpose of this book and of the Becoming More Model.

The way you tell your stories affects your mental health and overall well-being. People who tell their stories with a positive twist, taking responsibility for the bad along with the redeeming possibilities of change, tend to enjoy greater well-being. Conversely, telling stories with more negativity and drama correlates with lower well-being and self-esteem. McAdams went on to say that changing one's self-authoring style and focusing on a positive outcome or meaning are beneficial in many ways.

> *The most important*
> *person we tell our stories*
> *to is ourselves.*

Life is never problem-free, and a great story isn't either. The world is full of contrast. There are day and night, hot and cold, hard and soft, good and evil. We depend on contrast to show us what we like or don't like. It is through contrast that your desires are formed and your story becomes epic or tragic, easy or challenging. Contrast makes us stronger and allows us to show up as a victim, a villain or hero, a leader, a great mom or dad. Embrace the contrast and the challenge, for iron sharpens iron.

STORIES SHAPE OUR MEMORIES

The world we live in is shaped by stories we tell and the memories they leave. Each story has a beginning, a middle, and an end. Since you probably prefer stories about you to be told a certain way, in a positive light, why not determine now what the story will be?

Should you start at the beginning? Probably not. It really doesn't matter how your story began, for you cannot redo the past, nor is it contingent on the portion you wrote yesterday. What matters is that you keep evolving, etching into the mind of others what you would like them to remember about you. Stephen Covey, in his classic book *The 7 Habits of Highly Effective People*, taught us to always start with the end in mind. This is how I see it—thinking of our life from the end backward is truly forward-thinking. This may sound counterintuitive, but the way to retell your story is to imagine your desired future and what kind of person you aspire to be. Then begin changing the key components of your story to lead to that end result.

> *You can't go back and change*
> *the beginning, but you can*
> *start where you are and*
> *change the ending.*
> —C. S. Lewis

So what is the final story they will tell about you? How will it end? Write it down now. As much as you may not desire to think about it, write out your eulogy. Reduce it to a few attributes you desire to be known for. Then schedule what you will do to demonstrate those qualities, reminding yourself daily to *live a story* that demonstrates them.

Every day at 7:00 a.m. my phone sounds an alarm and across my screen pops the question, "What will you do today to add value to people?" At 7:00 p.m. the alarm sounds again and my screen displays, "What did you do today to add value to people?" This way, each day I am working intentionally to live the story that will be told when my time on this earth ends: "She added value and made a difference."

BECOMING MORE

We all have a purpose, a destiny, and a destination; it is up to us to get there.

> *In the end , we'll all become stories.*
> —Margaret Atwood

No matter the story running through your head, even if you are a victim of circumstances or a villain tearing yourself apart, it doesn't have to be the final edition. You can write a new account. You can be a person of victory—indeed, a hero—who overcomes many challenges. Go from success to significance by becoming a coach or mentor for others.

Every day you are planting seeds in your life from the stories you choose to tell. When you change the way you tell your story to yourself and others, you change your life . . . and the world around you.

> *You never change things*
> *by fighting existing reality.*
> *To change, you must build*
> *a new story that makes*
> *the existing story obsolete.*
> —Buckminster Fuller

It's time to rise up, for an eagle doesn't live in a sparrow's nest.

76

Start with the End in Mind. Write Your Eulogy.

Reduce it to what you desire to be known for.

_____

_____

_____

_____

_____

_____

_____

_____

_____

_____

_____

_____

_____

_____

_____

CHAPTER 6

YOUR JOURNEY TO MORE

All you need is the plan, the road map,
and the courage to press on to your destination.
—Earl Nightingale

The fact that you turned the page automatically means you've decided to move forward. You're on your way! You've picked up the pen and are ready to write a new story. As the creator, main character, crusader, and champion of your story, it will help to know the twists, turns, and terrain you will encounter on your inner journey ahead.

When it comes to your story, you are standing on a particular square of the gameboard of life based on the decisions you've made, not the hand you've been dealt or a roll of the dice. Even if you might not feel this way, it has been your choice every minute. Now you can learn how you made those choices and how you can start to make different ones.

BUCKLE UP

One writer who has helped me think about how our life stories typically play out is Joseph Campbell, who, in 1949, published the groundbreaking book *The Hero with a Thousand Faces*. In it, he walks readers through comparisons of the great mythological tales in what he calls the "Hero's Journey." This book made such a profound impact that it has become the de facto standard for Hollywood storytelling.

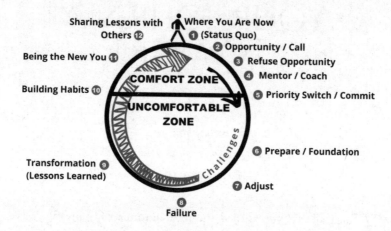

The Journey Model © Dianna Kokoszka

Figure 4: The Journey Model lays out a comprehensive map of the path you will follow through every chapter. Since each chapter delves into a unique facet of your life, you will embark on the journey from where you are now (Status Quo), repeatedly throughout the book. The journey may not be easy; however, it will be worth it.

The Journey Model works much in the same way—only we're going to talk about your one and only life, not the tale of a revered mythological figure. Think of this model as a journey, and along the way to your desired destination you will be stopping at little towns. These towns represent inward (psychological) changes that will bring outward results.

As you learn, implement, fail, learn, and implement again, you will find yourself closing the gap from where you are today to where you desire to be. This will be a simple twelve-choice journey and—when completed—you will find what was once the ceiling you were reaching for has now become the floor you stand on. You will then look up at another ceiling to get through . . . and the journey begins again. Like each new day, you begin anew.

Whether you realize it or not, we are all generally thinking and talking about where we are, where we've been, or where we are going. Sometimes we are caught up in the thought of how long we will stay in a particular place. We get stuck where we're at and need to get back in the car and drive to the next stop. Here is how to do that:

1. STATUS QUO. The first town is where you are right now, the present moment of your life where a new story is emerging. If you stay here, of course, nothing will change and you will grow old in this town, not seeing the bigger, wider world.

2. OPPORTUNITY/CALL. While in Status Quo, all of us will be presented with an opportunity, a calling. This could be to build a new relationship, make more sales, pursue a promotion, become healthier, tackle a specific challenge, or simply respond to a gut feeling that you desire to be more, do more, have more, and give more. You might simply be aware of a tension in your life. Deep down you know you have more promise than where you are, and this tension between remaining safe and comfortable and choosing to answer the call intensifies your desire.

It's much like driving the car while listening to jazz on the radio. You hear the flat notes that seem dissonant, then suddenly resolve to a note that sounds harmonious; your calling will be the same. You will have a little dissonance, disharmony, and tension to overcome from time to time. Just as the individual notes, the sharps and flats, your life will get *sharpened* (although you might feel *flattened* now and then) as you overcome trials along the way. This allows transformation to occur!

Where does the dissonance come from? There are countless ways we could respond to this, yet I believe most of our dissonance comes from four deep desires:

- **One** is the desire to improve your environment, which includes improving yourself—to become more, do more, have more, and possibly give more than you are now.

- **Two** is to be understood. For you to be understood, people must put themselves in your shoes and have empathy, asking you questions, tuning into your thought process, your mindset, and sometimes your energy. Without this happening, you may not feel like they truly understand you.

- **Three** is to be loved. Every person on earth desires to be loved. Some people think in order to love them you must understand them, but the two have nothing to do with the other.

- **Four** is to belong. Whether it is belonging to a group, a community, or a team, we all long to be part of something bigger than ourselves.

Your true identity and reason for being reside somewhere within your response to these desires. If any of the needs are not being met, the longing is what triggers the tensions we feel and causes us to desire to escape our status quo and seek other opportunities.

If a desire has been nagging in the back of your mind without you acting, you're most likely stuck in our next stop, the town of Refusal.

3. REFUSAL. This is a dangerous detour. You've decided you were happy with the streets of Status Quo, preferring familiarity over the opportunity to change. Think back through your life, anything you have desired and not yet obtained may have been by refusing the journey. Have you ever limited yourself, missing out due to thinking

I don't have a choice.

Of course, I want more—I just don't have what it takes.

People just don't understand what I'm going through.

I did that in the past and failed.

You may even be in the town of Refusal right now! In order to get out and avoid reverting back to your old ways of negative self-talk, you may need some help from a coach or mentor to change your oil to a "Positive Season" blend.

4. COACH OR MENTOR. They arrive in town and through questions or teaching, sometimes a combination of both, they refill your gas tank, motivating you to continue driving on. Sometimes your car is stuck, and you need a friendly push from an outside force. Seek guidance from others who have gone before you or are trained to guide, direct, ask questions, teach, and motivate you to get going again. Your responsibility is to bring the will and desire to implement the insights they help you discover, for change is always an inside job.

Along your journey, you might ask for directions. Be careful whom you listen to, for they may not know the way and you'll find yourself far from your desired destination. At each little town, you have the freedom to make choices, yet you cannot escape the consequences of the ones you make.

> *First we make a choice.*
> *Then our choices make us.*
> —ANDY ANDREWS

It isn't an accident you opened this book, whether you bought it or someone gave it to you. You are reading it for a reason. If you are looking for a sign to accept your call, this is it. For me, accepting a call meant putting my kids in a little red wagon (I couldn't afford a babysitter) and going door-to-door prospecting for real estate customers. From these meager beginnings, I eventually advanced to the C-suite as CEO, leading a team that built one of the world's largest coaching and training companies.

With the help of coaches and mentors, I learned many lessons. One is that through sacrifice, your new self emerges. You will have to give up your old habitual self to become more. As the actor F. Matthias Alexander said, "People do not decide their futures, they decide their habits and their habits decide their futures."

One of the major obstacles you will face is your natural tendency either to move away from pain or toward pleasure. These two controlling forces drive our human behavior and direct our life decisions. Which do you believe you tend to do? Are you sure?

Imagine that one evening you and friends decide to enjoy a campfire on the beach. You're having a great time, and as the sun fades, setting behind the water, it isn't long before you wish you had a jacket to ward off the cold night air. Desiring to warm up, you step closer and closer to the fire. Did you move toward the fire to gain the pleasure of warmth, or were you moving away from the pain of being cold? Because the majority of people are hardwired to do whatever they can to avoid pain instead of moving toward pleasure, I would submit that you moved closer to get away from the discomfort of the chilly air.

What if you are presented with two roads that are both difficult and painful yet equally important to you? How do you choose which is the priority? You have arrived at the town of Priority Switch.

5. PRIORITY SWITCH. This is probably the most important town of all in your journey. Here your brain switches back and forth between two different motivations, eventually choosing the road that presents the least difficulty and will cost the least to your emotions and psyche.

Let's say your friends want you to go out, yet you have work to do. The work assignment isn't due until next week, so you opt to avoid the pain of missing out on having fun. Later in the week, your friends invite you to a movie. The same assignment is due the day after tomorrow, and you haven't even started it yet! At this point, your brain pretty much flips the priority switch and makes the decision for you to immediately decline the invitation, because the pain of not having your work completed is now more intense than missing the movie.

This is an empowering town if you decide to explore it properly. You have the ability to switch your priority by choosing your own pressure points and identifying which will inflict the most pain. Take something in the future you are very excited to do and priority switch it by deciding you won't do it *unless* you accomplish a task you are not motivated to do. The pain of not experiencing what you desire will drive you to get through the pain of the unwanted task. Use the power of being able to measure your short-term pain versus long-term pain to make a switch.

Commitment then sets in big-time. You find yourself taking

decisive action to enter the uncomfortable zone of doing whatever it takes to achieve your goal. Welcome to Decision Point . . .

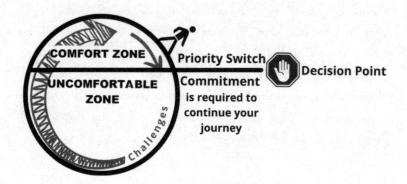

Priority Switch, The Decision Point Model © Dianna Kokoszka

Figure 5: The Priority Switch, The Decision Point Model signifies that you remain stagnant or move backward until you choose: embrace the comfort zone and accept its consequences or venture into unfamiliar territory, the uncomfortable zone.

When you stop at Decision Point, if you choose to back up, you will get a ticket that you will be paying off the rest of your life. If you drive through and beyond the Decision Point, however, you enter the uncomfortable zone. You will naturally resist the discomfort, but you have to keep your eye on the destination. An important word here is *decide*, the root of which means "to cut off." The moment you decide to move forward, you are cutting off all other options—and there's no turning back.

If you don't commit, you will repeat the process, hitting the top speed of your achievement or falling to a plateau lower than where you currently are. We all live in a cause-and-effect world where our choices determine our future. You have the agency to choose to continue on your journey or to allow a roadblock to stop your progress. The magnitude of this decision is so important. Our brain makes assumptions and judgments about almost everything. Often, it is our *perspective* of a particular pain or pleasure, not actual pain and pleasure, that drives us. Our expectations help determine our perspective, which we then use to prioritize the amount of pain we're willing to feel. To prevent this, all you need to do is change your perspective.

LONG-TERM PLEASURE OVER SHORT-TERM PAIN?

We've already talked about how we tend to move toward pleasure and away from pain. Now let's look at this fact under the lens of time. Do you go to the gym regularly? Then you understand long-term pleasure over short-term pain. You also have mastered one area of making the lack of great health and stamina more painful than the aching muscles you experienced from your workout.

What's important to remember is you will experience many, often conflicting road signs on your journey at the point of Priority Switch. The key to knowing these axioms is to understand where the potholes you will encounter are coming from. Though the road ahead may have curves and slow you down, understanding the pleasure and pain principles will take you to the town of Long-Term Pleasure. Once you are able to discern what's going on inside you, you can make better decisions and drive forward on the path to becoming more.

6. PREPARATION/FOUNDATION. You've adjusted your priorities and made your decision. Embarking on the unfamiliar terrain of the uncomfortable zone requires gathering additional supplies for the voyage ahead. As you get ready to set off, ensure that your bags are packed, your car is fueled, the oil is checked, and you have a spare tire; it's faster to prepare than wait for a repair.

> *By failing to prepare*
> *you are preparing to fail.*
> —BENJAMIN FRANKLIN

It's through preparation that you find yourself able to be comfortable with being *un*comfortable. Uncharted territories can bring on challenges. Your best ally will be preparation. The reverse of Benjamin Franklin's wise words is also true: *By succeeding in preparation, you are preparing to succeed.*

For example, your preparation may include engaging with a support group or inner circle that helps you create an environment in which you can thrive as you work on becoming more. That support is key, for without it, the man or woman in the mirror could end up being your greatest enemy as you work to improve yourself.

When you encounter detours on this part of your journey, take time to reflect on lessons they teach you, and build a strong foundation as you move into *becoming more*. No matter how much we might prepare, things don't always go to plan.

7. ADJUST. This is where challenges, setbacks, and breakdowns are followed by breakthroughs, successes, and advances. Learn how to handle both with humility, always being grateful *in* all things. Notice I didn't say be grateful *for* all things; that would be a little crazy. There will be things that happen you are not grateful *for*. Always keep an attitude of gratitude *in* those times, learning, adjusting, growing, and being flexible through them.

8. FAILURE. Contrary to popular belief, you cannot have a story of success without a story or two of failure. Success and failure are not on opposite ends; they are a two-lane road, side by side. We will all fail at something. Some people fail often. This is a normal part of the journey, and it's certainly not the end of it!

> *Success is not final,*
> *failure is not fatal:*
> *it is the courage to*
> *continue that counts.*
> —WINSTON CHURCHILL

It's interesting to me how many people only want to talk about their successes and victories, all the while knowing we connect faster and deeper by sharing our mistakes and lessons learned. We receive accolades for success, yet wouldn't we learn more if we also spoke of failure and what we learned from it? As a CEO I would often lead "Failure Friday" where people would speak of the lessons they had learned through failing.

You may not like to hear this, but you *will* fail. . . . Remember, true failure results only if you don't learn from mistakes and begin again with renewed determination and skill. When we learn, it is never a failure. Allow the wrong turns of your past to teach and motivate you to higher ground in the future. Don't live your life looking in the rearview mirror!

9. TRANSFORMATION. This is a wonderful scenic spot full of surprises! When you become comfortable in taking the journey up to this point, your transformation is powerful. You are making use of the lessons you have learned. Even though bumps in the road arise, you find you have developed shock absorbers, taking them on with elegance and ease. What once may have derailed you is now a mere speed bump on the road to becoming more.

10. BUILDING MOMENTUM. You are almost at your destination! Now you're getting comfortable with the challenges and setting a new normal, clearing the road for all you desire.

11. BEING THE NEW YOU. You have shed your old habitual self that limited you. Like getting a new car, you are proud to show others this better version of yourself. It's a smooth ride at last!

12. SHARING LESSONS. You have a road map others can now follow. As the hero of your story, you embark on being a coach or mentor. Through sharing lessons learned with humility, in service of others, helping them become more, you are in the midst of greatness. Remember those who have helped you along the way and honor them. First you get it, then you live it, then you give it.

Your journey never stops. You've become more as you've arrived in yet another town of Status Quo because you are not yet all you can be. Each time you become more, a new opportunity presents itself, and you start once again to make decisions that will move you upward, provided you become comfortable with being uncomfortable. If you choose to apply the brakes on this continuous journey, however, other cars will pass you by. You will feel as if you are going backward.

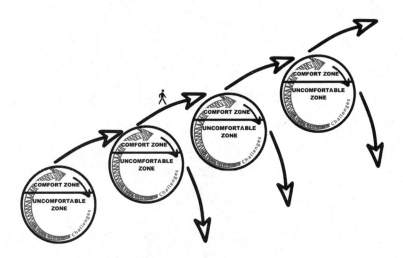

Journey Progression Model © Dianna Kokoszka

Figure 6: The Journey Progression Model reveals that embracing discomfort by entering into the uncomfortable zone propels you toward greater accomplishments, while staying within your comfort zone can lead to a decline from your current success.

This is how we move from block to block on the Becoming More Model. For the rest of this book, you will begin each chapter in the Status Quo of who you are being, and you will need to make a Priority Switch in each step. There will be things that will make you uncomfortable. Embrace this reality!

A mind, once stretched by a new idea,
never regains its original dimensions.
—Oliver Wendell Holmes Jr.

Let the journey begin!

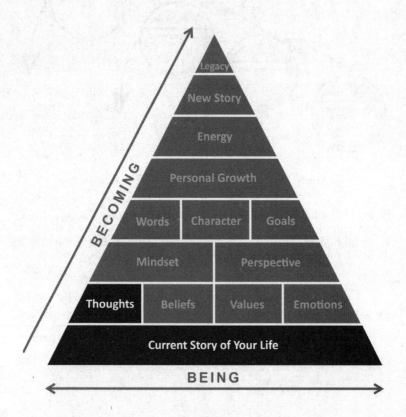

CHAPTER 7

THOUGHTS— NARRATIVES ON REPEAT

As a man thinketh, so is he.
—JAMES ALLEN (adapting Proverbs 23:7)

Everything created begins with a thought. It's a simple notion on the surface, yet a profoundly significant one. You will become keenly aware of the miracle of how mere *thoughts,* through implementation, become *actual, experiential, tangible things.* What was once an idea, a concept only imagined, can become a physical reality.

Walt Disney was known for his creative thoughts. After Disneyland, he had a bigger, better, and bolder thought. He couldn't feel it, couldn't touch it—others couldn't see it—yet it was totally alive in his mind. Indeed, it was so alive, and his thoughts were so imbued with passion, that their very articulation gave birth to an infectious vision that captivated those around him. Eventually, after years of relentless pursuit, that vision transformed his ideas into reality: a magical community all its own—*Walt Disney World.*

Sadly, while it was Walt's thoughts that launched this magnificent dream, he passed away before it was completed. At the ribbon-cutting ceremony for the park, it is rumored that one of the officials turned to Walt's wife, Lillian, and expressed what was probably on many people's minds:

"I wish Walt could have seen this."

"Oh, Walt saw it, or we wouldn't be here," she replied.

How true! For years he refined, shared, and pursued his vision. *He was just waiting for everyone else to catch up.* As a result, Disney World still stands as one of the great and continuing human achievements. It even has its own zip code!

You, too, have thoughts and dreams that could become a reality; grand projects you wish to undertake; great things you wish to build. Perhaps, instead of turning your dreams into reality, you have allowed those dreams to lie dormant, or maybe (and sadly) *you've already buried them.*

Have you thought about the possibility that the difference between you and Walt Disney may come down to how you manage your thoughts? Regardless of how many dreams you have buried, your future is absolutely wide open because, starting today, you can resurrect your thoughts, ideas, and dreams and take steps that will transform them from fantasies to realities. Your body or finances may be limited, yet your thoughts can unlock boundless horizons of exploration and discovery.

YOUR HABITUAL WAY OF THINKING

From the moment you enter the world as a "precious baby" without a care, you absorb the thoughts, words, and actions of others like a sponge, growing to imitate them. As time passes, television, friends, movies, social media, and the like invite themselves into your awareness.

As a child, did you ever watch a scary movie before being sent to bed alone? Were you afraid to go? Why? Because you were absolutely certain that something was lurking under your bed or in the closet, ready to attack the moment the lights went off. You didn't want to drift off to sleep! And in every instance, the thoughts and images you formed were programming your mind, giving birth to thoughts of fears—fears that were hard to shake, no matter how irrational.

Each encounter eventually becomes the programming for this miraculous computer system called your brain. Experience allows differentiation to set in, and the naive imitation you had as a child fades as you begin to form your own unique habitual thought patterns.

Here you are today—a person with many different thoughts: wonderings, questions, and doubts. You are still caught up in this process that never ends—bombarded moment to moment with information. Whether you are consciously paying attention or working actively *not* to pay attention, your brain still does, which has an effect on you. Whether it is getting dressed, driving to work, or walking into a restaurant, you continue to find yourself thinking and behaving the same way. Why?

The answer is the sheer *volume* of thoughts that race through your brain. Researchers and doctors have debated the exact number of thoughts we encounter in a day. It is somewhere between six and sixty thousand. Whatever the exact number, it's a lot! The problem, according to the National Science Foundation, is that on average, 80 percent of our thoughts are negative and 95 percent are the same thoughts you had yesterday, the day before that, and the day before that.

You must choose to actively break the habitual patterns of your thought life.

Are you known as a *big* thinker, or could your thinking use some help? Wherever you are in life right now is due to the category, size, and consistency of your habitual thoughts. Every area, whether personal, business, relationships, even money, is capped at the level of your thinking.

HERE, IN A NUTSHELL, IS HOW IT WORKS

Your brain is made up of billions of neurons transmitting thoughts through electrical impulses from one neuron to another via a pathway called an axon. Yes, dendrites and synapses and cell bodies are involved, yet the main point is the more you consciously or unconsciously allow that same thought to occur, the more the firing and wiring of your brain reinforces the strength of the pathway your thought travels along.[1]

Neuroscience tells us that nerve cells that fire together, wire together.

The familiar expression "We're hardwired that way" describes how we automatically think and behave. The more you have a thought, the more it is literally hardwired in your brain. The danger is that habitual thoughts can blind us to our own realities, preventing us from challenging old patterns that limit us.

Have you ever walked through a field or crossed a lawn in the same spot over and over again? A pathway is naturally formed. With time and repetition, this pathway becomes more established, forming a rut. The more you use it, the easier it is to *keep using* it. Eventually, it becomes so second nature to us that we forget this path is neither

---

[1] Dominique Debanne et al., "Axon Physiology," *Physiological Reviews* 91, no. 2 (April 2011): 555–602, https://pubmed.ncbi.nlm.nih.gov/21527732/.

necessary nor required, nor is it always the best route to take.

Your brain works the same way, always looking for ways to be more efficient. When you have the same thought, you consistently allow it to travel along the same axon, reinforcing the neural pathway. With enough repetition it becomes quite easy and even "automatic"; your brain quickly and surely travels the same way.

Notice I said *same* way rather than *best* way. Over time, these paths become ingrained and feel natural, even inevitable, *when nothing could be further from the truth.* Your habitual thoughts feel inescapable and, like the well-worn path, might ensure a certain safety and predictability—yet they won't take you anywhere new. A path can lead you somewhere desirable or undesirable, over and over again.

The good news (as we've already begun to explore) is that your brain can adapt and change. This flexibility, called *neuroplasticity,* provides another fundamental truth we can take from neuroscience:

Nerve cells that no longer fire together, no longer wire together.

Your brain isn't fixed in concrete. Like plastic, it can be molded, rewired, and reprogrammed to serve you better. New pathways can be formed, allowing new ways of thinking to emerge. Wouldn't it be great if we could do this instantly? Unfortunately, because of that voice we continually hear in our head, this can be challenging yet doable.

THE INESCAPABLE STORYTELLER

If you haven't noticed, you have a mental dialogue going on in your head. You may be saying to yourself, *What mental dialog?* That's the one I'm talking about! That inner voice I call your *inescapable storyteller* that resides permanently in your mind, living entirely rent-free. To be clear: I'm not talking about that still, small voice that so often brings you guidance and direction. Rather, this is the internal voice that is always present, always "on," always talking, putting limiting thoughts in your mind, whether you asked for them or not.

Often it can be a *Devious* storyteller, jabbering incessantly about your shortcomings.

You're not good enough.

You're not attractive enough.

Your body isn't the right shape.

You'll never be successful.

Even nighttime brings no solace as the storyteller reminds you of something you did or didn't do, should or shouldn't have said. The thoughts go on and on about your troubles—your children, that morning's fight with your spouse, the boss's snub at work—making you worry about things that may, or more likely may not, have any relevance to your happiness and success. The adversarial stories continue to pop into your head, swirling and twirling, picking up speed like an unstoppable tornado that can easily spiral out of control. Perhaps you work actively to dismiss them, ignore them, or dampen them from your conscious mind, yet your subconscious mind is still being impacted. While you believe you are not accepting the thought, you are accepting the beatdown of your spirit, your energy, and your character.

Of course, the opposite is also true. You might be under the control of a very different storyteller: the *Flatterer.* This one has you convinced that you are better than everybody else. Maybe you have accomplished a great deal in your life, or maybe your ego has convinced you of it. Either way, the brief emotional high you get from this flattery doesn't last long. You may find yourself depending on others to build you up with flattery for reassurance and acceptance. That's a slippery slope that almost always ends with narcissistic behavior and frustration as you ask yourself, *Why don't people listen to me? Why won't they do what I ask them to do? Why don't they support or respect me?* When these thoughts occur, we begin to act like a victim who complains or a villain upset at the world.

Sometimes there is a mixture. Have you heard either of these storytellers in your mind? Do you ever wonder why the storyteller relays stories that are negative and limiting, bringing defeat and inferiority—and then suddenly shifts to liberating and positive stories of success, moving to superiority? The stories can swing on the pendulum from negativity through positivity to narcissism. No wonder you feel vulnerable and insecure one minute and on top of the world the next!

Then there is the *Reasonable* storyteller. Maybe you hear this one more than the others. It understands you, sympathizes with you . . . and can create the most havoc in your mind. How? By dishing up reasons and excuses that you accept and take in like water on a hot summer's day. Since we can have either excuses or results, when we accept excuses, paralysis sets in, causing our tasks that need completion to sit undone.

Do you ever wonder who the inescapable storyteller is? The answer is surprisingly simple: *you*. You are doing the talking and you are doing the listening as you live out a negotiated, moment-to-moment existence within yourself. You are manufacturing the stories in which you play the heel or the hero, the victim or victor, the one giving reasons or achieving results. You are the ultimate thinker in your mind, with your thoughts fueling the stories you hear.

What stories are you telling yourself about yourself? About others? About your life and the world outside your head? Why do you tell these stories? One reason is that you have a buildup of energy inside of you that needs to come out. Maybe it is nervous or fearful energy, maybe it's the energy of excitement. Regardless, this contributes to the inescapable storyteller continuing to talk.

There is one more storyteller: the *Empowering* storyteller. It holds the potential to make you the hero of your own life and eventually the coach or mentor for others.

You *cannot* control all the thoughts the *Devious, Flatterer, or Reasonable* storyteller shares. You *can* control whether you continue to focus on or dismiss them. Your thoughts are like a fire and your focus is the gasoline or water you pour on them.

The better news is that, through the intentionality and discipline of stating declarations and affirmations, you can strengthen the *Empowering* storyteller's ability to combat the limiting thoughts shared by the other storytellers living in your mind as well as the stories you hear from outsiders.

Limiting vs. Liberating Thoughts

Limiting Thoughts	Liberating Thoughts
Devious/Flattering/Reasonable Storytellers	Empowering Storyteller Affirmations/Declarations
I'm not good enough	Every day, in every way, I'm getting better
Money is the root of all evil	Money is good for the good it can do
Problems bring hardship	Problems bring opportunity
I have too much to do	I prioritize, focus, and take action
I have to have a title to be a leader	I am a leader, even if I am only leading myself
Hard work is the only way I can get ahead	Intentional living gets me ahead
Things aren't going my way	Things are always working out for me
It can't be done	I am capable of completing the task
It's too hard	I can figure it out

*Go to Becomingmorebook.com/resources for more affirmations.

In his research, world-renowned psychologist Lev Vygotsky told us how vitally important our inner speech is. It starts at age three and continues to play a crucial role in regulating how we think and behave. We are constantly looking at the world with glasses tinted by our inner dialogue of positivity or negativity.

When it comes to negative thoughts, in no way am I saying you are wrong for having them. We all do. You just don't have to live your life in service of them. One of the first steps you can take to set yourself free is to recognize when you're having negative and self-limiting thoughts.

In his book *Change Your Brain, Change Your Life*, Daniel G. Amen, M.D., shares a very useful concept for identifying negative thoughts that limit us. He calls them Automatic Negative ThoughtS (ANTS).[2] There are different types of ANTS. Some are obvious and others more subtle. Maybe you recognize some in yourself or others:

- All-or-nothing thinking

- Focusing on the negative

- Fortune-telling—predicting the worst possible outcome

- Mind reading—believing you know why someone says or does something

- Thinking with your feelings

- Guilt—thoughts expressed in the well-known phrase "Woulda, coulda, shoulda"

- Labeling yourself or others negatively

- Blaming others for the problems you are facing (the most poisonous ANTS of all)

---

[2] Daniel G. Amen, MD, *Change Your Brain, Change Your Life* (New York: Crown: 2008).

When you couple your ANTS with emotion, they embed even deeper into your mind and, much like a prisoner of war, you are held against your will, bound by your thoughts. You must take your thoughts captive, for the greatest battles you fight are not against your environment or others; they are against the invisible thoughts you allow to remain in your mind.

If you picked up a jar that had ants all over it, what might happen? They would crawl from the jar right onto you. The same is true when you frequent people who continually share their Automatic Negative ThoughtS with you—their ANTS crawl right into your brain, foraging and feeding as they grow larger.

How can you get rid of those pesky ANTS? The answer boils down to your perspective. Looking for the positive in the situation and expressing gratitude will not only keep ANTS from building a hill of negativity; it will also exterminate them. For you cannot be grateful and negative at the same time.

WHAT YOU FOCUS ON EXPANDS

What do you think about most of the time? Your life will be big or small, geared toward wealth or poverty, depending on your most dominant thoughts. As James Allen reminds us, "Unhappy thoughts have a slew of unfortunate side effects . . . a higher heart rate, poorer sleep, headaches, and yes, wrinkles from all that frowning."

- Consistently think of creating wealth, and you will find ways to make money.

- Think of service, and you will find numerous ways to serve others.

- Focus on happy, positive thoughts, and you will become happier.

- Surround yourself with drama, and you'll continue to find more drama.

- Think of beauty, and it will find you.

In the California Gold Rush, people didn't look for the dirt; they looked for the gold. Focusing on gratitude is like finding gold. When you discover and hold up that precious nugget, all the dirt that is so easy to complain about dwindles away.

Evaluate your current circumstance in your life financially, personally, socially, and relationally. All of these reveal the current nature and level of your thinking. Are you thinking big enough? If you find yourself dissatisfied, borrow the wisdom that Zig Ziglar gave me: "If your thinkin' is stinkin' you need a checkup from the neck up." Align your thoughts with what you desire, then watch everything fall into place.

You are now and will always be a product of the thoughts you have. Each thought serves to confine or empower you. Consciously fostering positive thoughts while diminishing your negative ones generates momentum toward achievement and fulfillment.

*Your thoughts carry you wherever
you want to go. Weak thoughts
don't have the energy to carry you far.*
—Israelmore Ayivor

YOU HAVE A RELATIONSHIP WITH YOUR THOUGHTS

How can you understand the relationship between yourself and your thoughts? Think about what is going on between your ears as an ongoing play or performance in the theater of your mind. You are the creator, director, producer, lead actor, and stagehand. You are the one with the megaphone, the one who gets to decide what thoughts occupy center stage with the spotlight bright on them. You determine who gets lines and the most applause, which, by the way, you will furnish because, incidentally, you're also the audience.

You have the ability to prevent certain actors from taking the stage: those who restrict your potential, such as thoughts of comparison with others or thoughts that lavish you with insincere praise.

It's not for me to tell you how to think. My role is to point out that the *way* you think and the priorities you give each thought about yourself create patterns and behaviors resulting in how you show up. This is the challenge we all face as the writer and director working to marshal all these thoughts/actors playing out our stories in every corner of our minds.

If you desire to change your life, change the thoughts you use to build your life. You hold the power to direct and control your mind to whatever means you desire.

> *You are not a hostage of your past—you are the architect of your future.*

YOUR THOUGHTS BUILD CAGES

What if I told you that right now you are living in a cage of your own choosing? Would you believe me?

The bars of the cage symbolize your thoughts, the cage your comfort zone, and the paths outside the cage your opportunities to pursue freedom. Will you choose to remain locked inside, allowing your thoughts and fears to sabotage your greatness?

We are designed to be great,
yet we continually sabotage
ourselves by thinking
mediocre thoughts about
who we are and the
experiences we encounter.

Are you willing to stay in your cage of comfort and remain a hostage to your thoughts? You possess the ability to generate thoughts that keep you within the confines of comfort, much like the restrictive bars of a cage. You might choose to remain there because it protects you from things that frighten you— maybe the fear of financial insecurity that prevents you from imagining a new career? Or perhaps the fragility of an important relationship. It could be the fear of failure, or maybe even the fear of your own success.

True, there may be some cold comfort in not dealing with these challenging thoughts, yet can you honestly say you're happy sitting there in your cage of comfort, waiting for something to change?

Perhaps, to justify your acceptance of the status quo, you seek out others who have built their own cage and share your thoughts. The problem is, you and your fellow enablers stay in your comfort zones, complaining and commiserating, perpetuating your discontent, continuing to live in the past. You have become the victims of the rules you have placed on yourself.

*Until you heal the wounds
from the past, you will continue
to bleed into the future.*
—Iyanla Vanzant

There is good news, though! Despite the fact we have been hardwired to react swiftly to things we feel threatened by, real or imaginary, we can train our brains to be more intentional, more selective about the thoughts and stories we construct. A profound truth—indeed, a principle of life many do not wish to hear—is that everything you want and do not have is outside your comfort zone. To go after it, you *must* break the boundaries of the invisible cage you have so carefully built around yourself. My recommendation is that you take the advice of this anonymous person:

"Step so far outside your comfort zone that you forget how to get back."

You can start right now with how you think.

CHANGE YOUR THINKING, CHANGE YOUR STORY

*The world as we created it is a process
of our thinking. It cannot be changed
without changing our thinking.*
—Albert Einstein

Change can happen at the speed of thought. Skeptical? OK, yet you are already practicing this. I bet you have easily dismissed positive thoughts or comments about yourself and changed them to negative ones (maybe even a few times today). The opposite can also be achieved: flipping negative narratives to positive ones. To move forward, it's wise to accept the fact that you *do* have the power to change your thoughts.

Countless men and women have come to realize the only things in life we have control over are what we are thinking at this very moment and the action (or inaction) we take based on those thoughts. You will never control the first thought—it enters without resistance—yet you can control the thought that follows.

> *You don't suffer because you have thoughts.*
> *You suffer because you judge them,*
> *resist them, believe them, wallow in them,*
> *or identify with them.*
> —Unknown

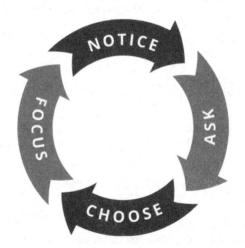

Thought Change Model © Dianna Kokoszka

Figure 7: The Thought Change Model offers a four-step process for changing your thoughts in real time.

FOUR STEPS TO TRANSFORM YOUR THOUGHTS

1. NOTICE a thought that is not serving you. Write it down. Put "thinking time" in your schedule and go through the next steps around that thought. You will be training your brain to eventually follow this model instantaneously.

2. ASK these questions:

If the thought is about you:	If the thought is about what is happening:
Who would I be without that thought? How would I feel without that thought?	Is it absolutely, 100 percent true? How would I feel without that thought? How do I act when I believe that thought? Who would I be without that thought? How would I feel without that thought?

3. CHOOSE the thought you desire to have. State an affirmation for that thought. An affirmation has to be in the present tense (I *am*, not I *will*) and be positive. Repeat it daily or even more often.

4. FOCUS on the new thought and new way of being.

As an example:

Notice: I am overwhelmed and anxious with all I have to do.

Ask: Who would I be without that thought? A happy person.

How would I feel without the thought? In control, calm.

Choose: I am a person who prioritizes my tasks and finalizes them quickly.

Focus: Prioritize a list and start moving forward. Of course, doing this once doesn't automatically change the way you think. It takes repetition. Think about it. A child who stays up late during the summer months rebels when they must go to bed at 8:30 p.m. the night before school. And you as a parent must take a stand for bedtime or your child will continue to rebel. Soon your child automatically knows 8:30 p.m. is bedtime. Your mind is no different. The habitual way of thinking that you have allowed and now desire to change will create some frustration and rebellion from your inescapable storyteller. As you think bigger and better, consistently, the empowering storyteller will take over and the others will turn to silence.

Your tomorrow is determined
by the thoughts you allow to
occupy your mind today.

Hold positive, successful thought patterns and you'll obtain massive success. If a thought has already moved from a mere thought to a deep-seated thought and you cannot shake it, we will address this in the next chapter, as it falls under the category of Beliefs.

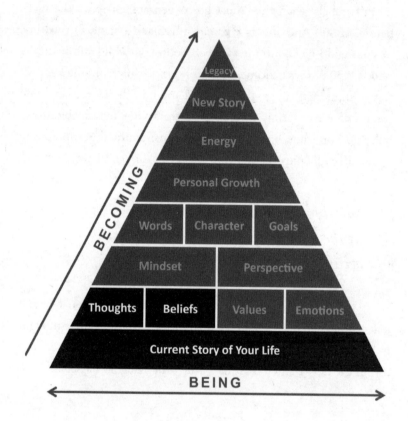

CHAPTER 8

BELIEFS—HANGING YOUR HAT

It's what you choose to believe that
makes you the person you are.
—KAREN MARIE MONING

Stepping out of my car into the chilled night air and wrapping my coat around me, I began walking toward the main gate. I was on my way to attend a motivational training seminar conducted by Tony Robbins. Looking back now, I'm not certain if the chill I felt was a result of the humidity and temperature or whether it had more to do with the fact that in a very short time I was going to be walking across white-hot coals—radiating immense heat—with my bare feet!

Once inside the auditorium, the energy was contagious and continued to build throughout the seminar. Throughout the night, we discussed the experience, wrote down and spoke about our fears, participated in guided meditation, and visualized the best outcome. In preparation to face the peer pressure of surrendering my thoughts to what was about to happen, my eyes focused on the ceiling as I practiced saying "cool moss," picturing it in my mind's eye—not hot coals but instead a soft carpet that was as easy to walk across as my own living room rug. If there were ever a situation that illustrated the truth of mind over matter, this was it! When the moment of truth came as I approached the fiery path, I knew the only way I would come out all right on the other side would be if my belief, faith, and trust were bigger than my fear of my feet being burned and scarred.

Notice the distinction. It wasn't about my attempting to eradicate every element of fear from my heart to move forward. I didn't have to be completely fearless to act. What I *did* need was to believe I would be OK. I had to decide which one—fear or faith—was going to "drive the bus." Which one of those realities would decide the way I went and how my future would unfold?

Fear or Faith . . .
the choice is yours.

Already having some semblance of my ability, my ears perked up when I heard the person in charge telling some attendees to move to the side since they were not ready to take the walk. When it was my turn, he allowed me to borrow his belief, reinforcing my own belief, as he said, "Look up, make a fist, and say 'cool moss.'"

I did.

"You're ready! Go now!"

Before I knew it, I had arrived on the other side. Yes, I made it! A sound that I can only describe as "sizzling" was heard as my feet stepped on the "damp grass." Mind over matter! Triumph over de feet!

You may never walk on hot coals, yet you will find yourself in situations where you have to decide whether to be driven by a strong belief that everything will be OK or paralyzed by fear. Making courageous choices does not require the absence of fear. Making brave choices is the decision to act in spite of your fears. It's the decision to believe and trust, choosing action over avoidance, motion over paralysis.

As my story illustrates, beliefs are powerful, almost mystical forces that have you trusting and showing faith or confidence in someone or something with unwavering conviction. While a belief feels overwhelmingly correct to you, it is not necessarily objectively true or universally applied to everyone.

In the previous chapter, we discussed how your thoughts can be grand or trivial, lasting or fleeting. They are cognition without commitment. It is when you start accepting your thoughts as representing the truth about reality, and you commit to them, that they become more than mere thoughts—they become your *beliefs*.

You might think the reason you believe something is because it is true, yet the real truth is you believe it because you've practiced, drilled, and rehearsed that thought over and over again. Do you remember our metaphor of comparing habitual thoughts to a pathway through a field? Frankly, a belief is a very well-worn pathway, one you trust and in which you have absolute faith.

BELIEF AND FAITH DIFFER

You also may think that faith and belief are one and the same. False; while faith includes an element of belief, they are not identical. A belief is rooted in the idea that something is true; it is a state of BEing. Faith is more than mere thought; it is a deep conviction, something you HAVE. Couple these two with trust, which is something you DO, and you have a winning combination.

Did you ever stop to think that your belief is centered in faith and your faith is centered in trust? When you believe in yourself, you have faith in yourself and so you trust your decisions. Belief is the foundation; the only way to lose faith or trust is to change your belief or stop believing altogether.

Belief is being, trust is doing, and faith is having.

These factors influence your inclination to take risks—or play it safe. Ultimately, while you make decisions with all three in mind, belief is the most dominant. Therefore, your beliefs around money, health, family, relationships, and spirituality predict your decisions that lead you down the path of success . . . or hinder your potential.

The beliefs that hold us back are often based on a distorted reality, yet in our mind we take those beliefs as truths, sometimes stating them as fact, especially to ourselves. Beliefs such as "I am not good enough" or "I'll never be able to make the money I desire" or "I can't find talented people to hire" are not true, yet too often we live as if they are. When you begin to discern your own beliefs and realize that what you believe about yourself may not actually be fact, you can begin to see where your beliefs either limit or liberate you.

Limiting beliefs place you in the victim role of your story. Acting on those beliefs makes you the villain sabotaging yourself, stealing your accomplishment toward success. Changing them to liberating beliefs makes you the hero, and acting out those liberating beliefs can eventually make you capable of being a coach or mentor.

No matter what you have been taught, your beliefs are a choice and a powerful motivator to act. Did you ever consider that some of your beliefs are under the surface of your awareness, hidden in your subconscious mind? They show up in what you say and do because they are ingrained in your character.

MISPLACED FAITH IN AN UNWORTHY BELIEF

You might recall that as a young girl I continually believed I was like Wonder Woman. One day, I climbed to the roof of our home, with rope in hand, intending to lasso the tree below. I pictured myself sliding down the rope to the ground to meet my parents by the car. Looking up, my mother screamed, "Get down off that roof *now!*"

My belief was I could be like Wonder Woman. That belief, while sincere, was also sincerely wrong! Little did I know in the showdown between my mistaken belief and gravity, I was no match—gravity would win. Sometimes an encounter with facts can be a rude but necessary awakening. Our beliefs can be quite profound, even if they are revealed to be quite flawed.

To spin off a wise old quip from former US Secretary of Defense James R. Schlesinger, "You are entitled to your own beliefs. But you are not entitled to your own facts."

The reason beliefs are so powerful and difficult to change is that they develop over a lifetime. The two prominent sources of our beliefs are our upbringing and our experiences.

From an early age your beliefs are molded by the influence of your parents, caregivers, and other authority figures in your life. You grow up "breathing them in," making them as natural as the language you speak. They can be empowering or restrictive, positive or negative, or a combination of both. Over time, these beliefs seem like your own convictions of reality, and you become so deeply invested in them that you begin to regard them as facts beyond question. It's crucial to acknowledge what we commonly perceive as facts are often not grounded in research and truth but, instead, in our personal histories and experiences, which may contain both genuine truths and potential distortions caused by misinformation and dysfunction.

There is a wonderful research experiment related to the power of our beliefs documented in the book *The Road Less Traveled* by M. Scott Peck. A marine biologist placed a shark into a large holding tank and released several small bait fish into it. As you would expect, the shark quickly swam around the tank, attacking and eating the smaller fish. The marine biologist then inserted a strong piece of clear fiberglass into the tank, creating two separate sections. She then put a new set of fish in the section where the shark couldn't reach.

Nevertheless, the shark quickly attacked. This time, it slammed into the fiberglass divider and bounced off. Undeterred, it kept repeating this behavior every few minutes to no avail. Meanwhile, the bait fish continued to swim around unharmed in the second partition. (They got the less perilous assignment.) Eventually, about an hour into the experiment, the shark gave up.

The scientist repeated the experiment several dozen times over the next few weeks. Each time, the shark got less aggressive and made fewer attempts to attack the bait fish. Eventually, the shark got tired of hitting the fiberglass and simply gave up and stopped attacking altogether.

Then the marine biologist removed the fiberglass divider, and what do you suppose happened? If you thought the shark did not attack, you're right. In fact, he didn't even swim to the other side of the tank. Through conditioning, the shark adopted a belief so strong that, even when his environment changed, he believed a barrier remained between him and dinner. What could his false belief cause? Starvation!

I submit to you that you are subject to the same kind of conditioning when you believe that you've run into an invisible wall—holding beliefs with conviction around your lack of something, maybe your intelligence, beauty, charisma, or worth as a person—and become convinced that these are actual barriers preventing you from enjoying an abundant life. On what do you base these limiting beliefs? Perhaps in your past you received negativity from somebody you trusted. You were told you weren't good enough, or it was insinuated very strongly. That person's words were like the glass divider in the shark tank, limiting you by inhibiting your confidence.

Even though that was a long time ago and the fiberglass divider has been lifted, you may still not believe there is a big ocean of "fish" (opportunities) out there for the feeding. Like the shark in the lab, you may believe you will always have the same results, encountering setbacks no matter what you do. You are allowing your past to define you, acting like your rearview mirror has become your windshield. You now believe that the barriers actually exist "out there," when in reality they exist only in your mind.

A limiting *thought* is like the shark hitting the barrier once or twice. A limiting *belief* is like the shark hitting it over and over again, resigned to the fact it is true. Each belief you hold is either a limiting belief holding you back or a liberating one moving you forward. It's tempting to believe people who have accomplished a great deal do not experience limiting beliefs. Don't fool yourself—even high-achieving people have them crop up from time to time. As you move upward at every level (even the very top), new actions are required, and with each new action, a new level of belief must precede it.

RECOGNIZE YOUR LIMITING BELIEFS

Ever wonder why they are called limiting beliefs? Because that's what they do . . . they limit us. One of the best ways to recognize your limiting beliefs is to be aware of your emotions. Anytime you feel nervous or anxious, there is generally a limiting belief lurking in your subconscious. But trust me, there is also an opposite liberating belief living on the other side that you can tap into.

Another helpful way to recognize whether you are experiencing more limiting or liberating beliefs is to read through the following chart. As you see the different examples, stop and ask yourself, *Which of these beliefs live inside my own head?* Mark all that you believe should apply. Not mere thoughts, the ones you actually believe.

Limiting vs. Liberating Beliefs

Limiting Beliefs	Liberating Beliefs
Mistakes must be avoided or hidden. I speak only of my successes so I can look good and be right.	Mistakes are how I learn a better way to do something. Sharing them at the appropriate moment with people I trust is a way to connect with others.
I can't find the right people to do the job I need to have done.	I know specifically what I'm looking for and work daily to find the right people.
I'm not good enough to do what great people do.	I am creative, resourceful, and whole, which allow me to achieve success.
I need the approval of others to succeed.	Because I approve and believe in myself, I'm able to succeed.
Difficult and sensitive conversations are challenging, so I avoid them.	I have the confidence to be emotionally honest with others, helping to move them forward.
I will study leadership when I have a team or I'm given a title.	I am a leader even if I only lead myself, so I study leadership to grow into opportunities.
I won't get the top jobs because I didn't go to college.	I am able to move ahead based on my results.

Which column is most descriptive of where you are right now? Which prevails: limiting beliefs or liberating beliefs? If there are more marks on the liberating side—great job! If you have many or even one limiting belief, let's work together to change them. I believe you deserve much more in your life!

Choose a limiting belief you marked and ask yourself the following:

- When did I first decide to accept that limitation as truth?

- How long have I held this belief?

- Who would I become without the belief?

- What would happen if I stopped believing it?

- What would happen if I gave myself permission to believe the opposite?

PUT IT DOWN

It was Cabo, Mexico, where I took the stage to speak about the power of our mindset in determining around 90 percent of our success. I asked for a volunteer, and a man named Shawn joined me on stage. I asked him to hold a glass half full of water out in front of him with his arm fully extended.

The audience expected me to deliver a parable about being an optimist seeing a glass as half full or the pessimist with the glass half empty. (Maybe a curious person wonders where half of the water went, and the realist says it still needs to be washed!) That is not what I had in mind. Instead, I asked Shawn how heavy the glass felt.

"Feels pretty light. It can't weigh but a few ounces," Shawn answered.

"OK, please keep holding it out in front of you, with your arm extended," I said, and turned back to the audience.

As I continued to speak to the crowd on limiting beliefs, Shawn stood tall with his arm positioned out in front of him, listening intently. Time crept by for Shawn as his arm began to drop ever so slightly until finally, he needed to stabilize his arm by placing his other arm under his elbow and propping up the one holding the glass. After about five minutes, his arm was cramping and starting to shake. I knew if he kept holding the glass much longer, his arm could go completely numb and he'd drop it.

"How heavy is the glass now?" I asked him.

"Heavy!" Shawn answered quite emphatically.

Did the glass actually gain weight over time? Of course not. The length of time he held the glass made it feel far heavier and more painful to hold. What first seemed inconsequential eventually became debilitating.

Your limiting beliefs work in the same way. At first, they don't seem to matter. Thinking about them a few times may not be that big of a deal, yet over time, they become more and more challenging until you feel powerless against them.

C. S. Lewis observed, "It's not the weight of the load that weighs you down, it is the way you carry it."

Don't keep holding on to your limiting beliefs like Shawn held the glass of water. Put the glass down. Break through the invisible barriers you have created of your past, break through your limiting beliefs, and give yourself a magnificent smorgasbord of opportunity and success! What you believe about yourself is what you will become, so believe the very best. After all, if you do not believe in yourself, chances are no one else will either.

While recognizing and understanding your limiting beliefs is crucial, my focus lies primarily on cultivating empowering beliefs within you. By embracing liberating beliefs, your life becomes boundless and filled with infinite possibilities.

A very graphic illustration that helped me realize how devastating limiting beliefs can be comes from a parable called "How to Kill a Wolf in Alaska." Knowing that the scent of blood attracts a wolf, Alaskan hunters developed a simple trap to get rid of them. They dip a knife in blood and then freeze it. After repeating this process several times, a thick popsicle forms around the knife and they secure it to a tree. The wolf smells the blood and automatically licks the popsicle believing it's a good treat. You can guess the rest of the story.

Your limiting beliefs may be undermining you—maybe not as harshly as for the wolf, where a wrong belief leads to its demise. But are your limiting beliefs causing you some inconvenience? Squeezing your bank account? Keeping you from success? The little stories you have internalized and believe about your limitations are as hard to resist as the scent of blood is to the wolf.

Take heart: you *can* learn to identify the belief you have around the scent and stay away from it! One practical way to start is by forgetting the "likes" (or the lack of them) you receive on social media. Basing your beliefs on that fleeting measurement can quickly contribute to the creation of limiting thoughts. Focus, rather, on what allows you to become all you can be, not what limits you.

> *You wouldn't worry so much*
> *about what others think of you*
> *if you realized how seldom they do.*
> —ELEANOR ROOSEVELT

RAISE YOUR EXPECTATIONS

When you raise your expectations and standards for what you expect from life, your life changes. Now, it would be simplistic and false to argue that you can do anything in the world if you just believe you can. Nevertheless, experience teaches us unequivocally that you absolutely will *not* be able to do it if you don't believe you can.

When you set your goals, do you honestly believe you deserve to obtain them? Note: I didn't ask whether you could achieve them, I asked whether you believed you *deserved* to obtain them. Too often we are held back because we do not feel worthy of reaching our goals. And if anything is certain, it is that you have to believe you deserve to achieve your goals and realize your dreams in order for either to happen.

For example, there is a financial thermostat inside your subconscious mind that regulates the amount of money you believe you deserve to make. I have to ask you, "What is the amount on your thermostat?" High or low, the answer is based on your beliefs. Like the thermostat in your home adjusting the temperature, your subconscious mind controls and adjusts your financial thermostat, allowing you to produce only what you believe you deserve. When you start to approach or go over what you believe you deserve, you may find yourself sabotaging your success, making certain you do not cross the imaginary line you've so carefully set as your deserved compensation. You work hard yet never enjoy the results because you don't believe you truly deserve them. You have to believe you deserve what you want to achieve.

To get even more specific, think about the income you made last year. Now think about what would happen if you made that in one month! What about one week? One day? One hour? That may be too far-fetched for you to fathom, but why? There are people in the world who make that kind of money, so why not you? And before you allow your reasonable storyteller to take over the conversation in your head, I want you to realize that the only way to set your financial thermostat to a higher amount is to believe you deserve more, allowing your mind to expand and think bigger.

To drive this point home, one of the exercises I created in 1995 showed a sample checkbook register within the students' workbooks. They were instructed to enter $1,000 as a deposit—then they had to "spend" all of it that day. The next day they received $2,000 of imaginary money and once again had to spend it, this time only on items they had not purchased the day before. Each day the amount continued to double—$4,000, $8,000, $16,000—and each day they had to spend the entire amount on new items. How many days do you think you could go? Work the exercise and see what day you stop. On day seven, you'd be spending $64,000 on new items. Could you do that? How about spending $512,000 on day ten? At what point do you stop? This exercise accomplished one thing for certain with those that completed it, and it could do the same for you: *expand your beliefs of what is possible.*

Please do not believe that I feel money is what makes you successful; I don't. I believe you make money to take care of yourself, your family, and to give to others. Money is good for the good it can do, and when you give to help others, it is very good!

The fact is you can develop liberating beliefs by creating new pathways for your thinking by stating *affirmations.* Affirmations are written in the positive present tense and said multiple times a day. Connect them with a present habit—such as when you eat. For example, look at the preceding "Limiting vs. Liberating Beliefs" table. The right column lists wonderful affirmations; you may also write your own. You can also go to Becomingmorebook.com/resources for additional affirmations. Affirmations stated over and over again hardwire those thoughts within your mind, eventually turning them into beliefs.

Cultivate beliefs that are so alive in your mind it seems they already exist. Believe in yourself as well as your goals and dreams, and at the same time, be grateful and live every day as though your dreams are actually taking shape—not *going* to take shape at some future time. They are taking shape in the present!

You must believe in yourself before you can value yourself. And you must value yourself in order to value and add value to others. So, onward to Values!

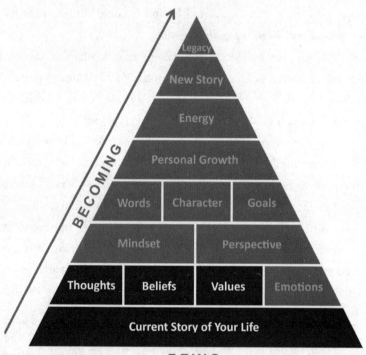

CHAPTER 9

VALUES—WHAT REALLY MATTERS?

Values are like fingerprints: nobody's are the same,
but you leave them all over everything you do.
—ELVIS PRESLEY

Once on a trip to Germany with my sister Raelene, I found myself with an entire day to tour Berlin while she worked at the world's largest travel trade show representing Ski Utah. My tour guide grew up during the Cold War, a time when the communist government of the German Democratic Republic (GDR, or East Germany) began to build the "Antifascist Bulwark" separating East and West Berlin—better known as the Berlin Wall. His family lived on the East (communist) side. As we walked along the remaining portions of the massive barriers, through the sandy portions where guards used to perch high in their stations watching for people to make a mad dash for freedom, he told me the following story.

Before the wall was built, his father had been a traveling salesman who regularly visited towns around Berlin for weeks at a time before returning home. One day, as he made his way through the city, he found himself confronting a system of barriers that would be part of the new wall. The barriers actually included two walls—the outer *Vorderlandmauer*, which stood eleven and one-half feet high, and the inner *Hinterlandmauer*, six and one-half feet tall. He was told by the guards that he now had to decide. He could remain outside the wall on the West, where he could enjoy his freedom and make a living for his family, only being allowed to cross into the East to visit them a few hours every month. Or he could live with them on the East side and work for the Communist Party. He chose to stay on the West side thinking it would only be a short while before he could be home again with them. Little did he know it would be twenty-eight years, two months, and twenty-seven days later. Each month he would visit them for a few hours, entering through Checkpoint Charlie, the infamous crossing point between the two Germanys. If he failed to check out at the appropriate time from East Germany, he would be forced to live there and face punishment.

What stood out for me was that providing for his family and being able to afford more than bare necessities under harsh Communist conditions was a stronger value than being present with his family. He must have experienced an immense inner conflict. I felt moved that his son, my tour guide, chose to honor his legacy by telling me his story.

You may also find yourself experiencing an inner conflict of values, albeit probably not as intense as the one my guide's father faced. For you, the value of achieving your career or financial goals may come into conflict with your value of being present in your family life. Or the value you place on physical health may be threatened by the pull of unhealthy habits. Know that the strongest value will always win out. If you learn to live with good values, however, life gets better. In fact, having good values is a reflection of how much you also value yourself. As we will see in the chapter on character, researchers are increasingly discovering that classic virtues lead to a more fulfilling life.[1]

*Values light the pathway
of your lifelong journey.
They determine the decisions
you will make that drive your life story.*

My walk through Berlin was eye-opening. Going through Checkpoint Charlie, taking pictures, and reading the history, I remembered a story from John C. Maxwell's book *Think on These Things*. One day, people who lived on the East Berlin side took a truckload of garbage and dumped it on the West side. The people of West Berlin could have retaliated by doing the same thing. Instead, they took a truckload of canned goods, bread, and milk and neatly stacked it on the East Berlin side. On top of the stack of food they placed a sign: "Each gives what he has."

Since we cannot give what we do not have, it only makes sense that your values will dictate what and how much you contribute to others.

SUCCESS IN LIFE MEANS LIVING BY YOUR VALUES

What does the word *value* mean to you? Did your mind go toward the values that display your character or the value you give to things in your life? For example, if you had the choice between water or a Coke, which would you choose? Some would say if you valued your health, water would win, yet if you valued the taste of Coke, it would

---

[1] The Positive Psychology Center at the University of Pennsylvania is a wonderful resource to find more about research into the "science of happiness." Visit https://ppc.sas.upenn.edu/.

win. What if the choice was water or Pepsi? Pepsi or Coke? Whatever you value the most will always prevail, even if you have to pay more.

So it only stands to reason that if you value people, you will add value to them. When it comes to people, John Maxwell told me, "If you see a person as hurting, you will help them; if you see them as broken, you will fix them; but if you see them as valuable, you will serve them."

Values are essential for transformation. The right values instill confidence, strength, and fortitude. This is why it is important to teach values to children. When kids have good values, they need less validation from others, but when they lack values, they require more validation—and often don't care where or from whom they get it.

In 2019, psychologists devised a clever experiment to test how adults influence the way a child approaches tasks. Preschool children watched an adult work to open a box and get at a toy hidden inside. Then, they were handed a box, but they didn't know that opening their box would be impossible.

Children who saw an adult succeed after much effort were more likely to persist longer in their own efforts. Even more, if they saw the adult make explicit value statements while opening their box— such as "Working hard is important!"—they were even more likely to persist in their own struggle longer.[2]

In my travels to many countries with Maxwell Leadership Foundation, I've been privileged to experience the results of Transformational Tables. The values-based educational programs are facilitated in schools and businesses. Values are *taught* and then *caught* at these events. One boy, fourth grader Pablo, spoke of how another boy pushed him down onto the pavement during a soccer game.

---

[2] Leonard, J. A., Garcia, A., & Schulz, L. E. (2019). How Adults' Actions, Outcomes, and Testimony Affect Preschoolers' Persistence. Child Development, 91(4), 1254–1271.

"The boy wanted me to forgive him, but I didn't want to because he had meant to hurt me," Pablo said. "But the next day I understood that we have to learn to forgive. So then I forgave him and we remained good friends."

The value of forgiveness enabled Pablo and the other boy to overcome a momentary setback to maintain a lasting friendship. Through my experiences, I have come to realize the significance of values and how they should never be underestimated.

> *It's not hard to make decisions*
> *when you know what your values are.*
> —Roy Disney

Many people prefer to gather around a table and talk strategy, thinking that will alleviate stress and create a more unified team. Though that is good, it doesn't go far enough. As the CEO of a large organization, discovering values was part of the interviewing process for me. Each candidate who would work in a role under my leadership was provided a list of values from which they were asked to select their top ten. After we talked for a few moments about these values, I asked them to narrow the list down to five. The purpose wasn't to eliminate them from being hired but to see how quickly they completed the exercise and to determine how certain they were about the makeup of their core values.

When people honor the values of one another, great things happen. People also learn values from the people they spend time with—and they learn how to live those values out better. Each team member knew the company's values, my personal values, and one another's values. With aligned values, you experience contentment, happiness, and a sense of belonging. Energy follows when a leader's personal values align with the values of an organization. The same can be true in a family, among friends, in a charitable organization, or in an extracurricular group.

PLAYERS AND PRETENDERS

One day my twenty-four-year-old grandson Armando and I were discussing the importance of values. He said, "You can live your life as an example, or you can live it as a warning." That is so true, and it has really stuck with me.

You separate players from pretenders when it comes to living out values. Over the years many companies have had "integrity" written on a wall in big letters for all to see. But do they live by that value? Often, these same companies have been embroiled in scandal—some even collapsed. They are pretenders, not true players.

The same goes for individuals. Some people compartmentalize their integrity, being honest only when it's convenient. Have you ever known someone willing to barter their integrity because it had a cost benefit attached? Likewise, many people have wonderful skills yet lack inner values. Skills are not enough to make someone a great person, let alone a great team member or leader. Without values, people work to manipulate and take advantage of one another— hardly leadership qualities!

When you become recognized for embodying certain values, your reputation spreads. For instance, my stepson, Todd, aspired to become an ornithologist, so he visited the University of Florida, widely known for expertise in that field. The head of the ornithology department at the university advised him that the only lucrative career option in ornithology was to obtain a PhD and teach at a university. This man knew Todd might also be interested in becoming a pilot.

So as an alternative, he recommended Todd pursue a pilot's degree at Embry–Riddle and treat ornithology as a passion rather than a profession. We still talk about the admirable integrity of this man to this very day and share his story with others. Thanks to him, Todd is currently a pilot for UPS and says he is "living his dream."

BECOMING MORE WITH VALUES

The thoughts you continually entertain build into a belief. But get this: That belief then acts as a gatekeeper for new thoughts and experiences, welcoming those that conform to the belief and denying access to those that refute or challenge its legitimacy.

This reinforcement of a belief eventually develops into a *value*. A value is more than a "rule" because it grows much deeper in our brain until it becomes a personal conviction.

Most people think beliefs and values are the same thing. While it's true that both guide and direct your actions, there are a few key differences. Beliefs are what you hold to be true, sometimes even without proof. Values operate as standards that designate the traits and qualities you view as most important in life. That's why you can have very different beliefs from another person but hold similar values. When our values are different, conflict can arise. And when our most precious values are challenged, our emotions flare up. It's only natural! It's no wonder that we can exist amicably and productively with people who do not share our *beliefs* but have a much harder time building close relationships with people who do not share our *values*.

This tension goes to show the role values play in growth and satisfaction. As illustrated in the following diagram, the closer a person is to you, the more important complementary and compatible values are to your feelings of contentment, happiness, and a sense of belonging.

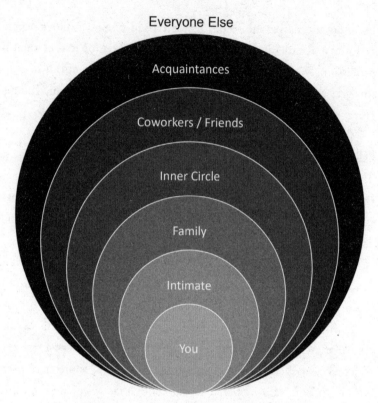

BECOMING MORE

Everyone Else

Acquaintances

Coworkers / Friends

Inner Circle

Family

Intimate

You

Compatible Values Model © Dianna Kokoszka

Figure 8: The Compatible Values Model shows the closer the person is to you, the more the values need to align.

VALUES DIFFER FROM MORALS

Just like Beliefs differ from Values, so, too, do Values differ from morals. Morals are specific, context-driven rules that drive you to take certain actions. Your morals will be governed by your values. If you value friendship, you probably see helping a friend in need to be morally right. However, if you value achievement more than honesty, your morals may say it's OK to cheat to get ahead.

VALUES—WHAT REALLY MATTERS?

In the movie *John Q.,* the main character's son needs a heart transplant to live. The hospital will not admit the boy because the family has no insurance. In desperation, John Q. takes hostages in the hospital and threatens the medical staff with a gun until they help him. But he never actually hurts them. Why? John Q.'s morals dictate honoring the sanctity of life. Throughout the movie, we watch his inner turmoil as he works to save the life of his son whom he values, in the only way that seems available to him.

Values give meaning to life and exert a big impact on our decisions, behavior, and actions—and it's not always a positive impact. In fact, the most common cause of stress and unhappiness is living our lives in conflict with our values. If your workplace values uncompromising loyalty and sacrifice in getting the work done on time, while you value a healthy work–life balance, you will begin to resent your company even if it is paying you well. This is because its values conflict with your own personal values. These inner conflicts can sometimes create such turmoil that one day we make a rash decision: we quit, and we can't even make sense to others as to why.

CHOICE POINTS

Every day you make far more decisions than you likely realize, all based on your values. Picking up that coffee on your way to work or getting up a few minutes early and making your own in order to save money? Binging on Netflix or going to the gym? Having food delivered or making a healthy meal at home? Having quality conversation with family or scrolling on your phone?

Therapists call these small decision moments "choice points." They happen when you must choose behaviors that are consistent or contrast with your values. Your values will always provide the compass pointing you in the direction to move.

CORE VALUES

Values help you act more assertively, communicate with more compassion, and increase your confidence. Some values may shift in importance as you go through the passages of your life, yet some will be lifelong and firmly established. These are your *core values* that will give your life its most profound meaning. They are the values that point your compass to your True North (your true self) and, when exercised, make you feel great on the inside. Every person has about five to seven core values without which they would become judgmental and even discontent with life.

> *Without clear core values,*
> *you can spend your life building*
> *an organization or a family*
> *that doesn't reflect what*
> *matters most to you.*
> —LORI CHAMPION

Ask yourself what values you need to hold to become the person you desire to be. In doing this the answers helped me redirect the priorities of my values. For example, success was important to me when starting my business. After all, making money and keeping the doors open were important. Then realizing to become the person I desired to be, it was necessary to change from *success* to *significance*. As a result, my focus changed to adding more value to others, helping *them* succeed. I love this quote from Billy Hornsby, the father of my friend Tammy Hodges:

*Some of my greatest accomplishments
in life were someone else's.*

Keeping my values posted in my office and looking at them daily reminded me what I stood for and desired to be known for. Doing this will help you understand how vital your core values are in every decision you make in life, how you lead your life, your mannerisms and style, and what career paths you have chosen. Your values associated with *growth* determine what courses you take in school, what jobs you eventually secure, whether you start businesses or seek to be employed, whether you stick to tradition or travel unbeaten paths.

LIMITING OR LIBERATING VALUES

Values are very often context-driven and interdependent on one another, which is why the same value that could be liberating might also be limiting. For example, let's say you value money because it empowers you to be generous (another value) and create opportunity (another value). But you could value money to such a degree that you hold on to it due to excessive self-love, closing your hand to others, refusing to let go of what you have. In that case, fear is driving *how* you value money. The same could be said about health. You choose whether it's a liberating or limiting value every time you eat!

In the diagram below, each value may be limiting or liberating depending on how you apply it. It would be best for you to think carefully about which of the values you currently hold. Each value will restrict or guide you toward growth. This could even change over time. For this reason, I've left the table with the value in the middle for you to determine which side the value belongs on for you, limiting or liberating.

Limiting Values and Liberating Values

Limiting Values	Liberating Values
← Money →	
← Health →	
← Achievement →	
← Loyalty →	
← Integrity →	
← Generosity →	
← Growth →	
← Family →	
← Fun →	
← Creativity →	
← Legacy →	
← Recognition →	
← Respect →	

To further illustrate the point, let's take three people with the same core value, *respect*. One only shows respect to others—their property, their friendship, time, and money—yet seems to have very little respect for themselves. They always put others first. The second expects everyone to show respect to them by doing what they want, when they want, judging people on how much respect they adore them with. The third balances a healthy level of respect for themself and for other people. For the first two individuals, respect is a limiting value, while the third is applying respect in a more liberating manner. The value of respect can, therefore, be limiting or liberating, depending on how you utilize it.

FULFILLING CORE VALUES

So how do you get yourself moving in a new direction that fulfills your core values? The key is to revise the choices you are making around values that are limiting you, preventing you from moving forward and accomplishing your goals. They sabotage your convictions and best intentions.

To fully maximize a liberating value, you must first understand it and articulate it effectively. This helps to make it a conviction. Once you have done so, you will find yourself able to achieve the necessary tasks toward success as your values allow you to set your priorities and supercharge your willpower.

Author and researcher Meg Selig has found that women who place a high value on the health of their baby during pregnancy are more likely to end bad habits that could affect the baby, such as drinking and smoking. This is one example that shows us that by aligning choices with values, our willpower is able to kick into gear.

Mark Muraven, a psychologist, once assessed the willpower of a group of participants in two ways. Both groups were given a series of frustrating puzzles. The first group was told, "Your work could help create new therapies for Alzheimer's disease," while the second group was told, "Try your best." Can you guess which group was best able to solve the puzzles? Obviously, it was the first—which showcases how the value of helping others gave purpose to what was a frustrating task and increased the willpower to accomplish it. When your willpower kicks in, you can win at things you never thought you would even compete in.

KNOWING, SHOWING, AND GROWING YOUR VALUES

Research consistently shows that knowing your core values brings many benefits, giving you the willpower to persist through tough times, build relationships, reduce stress—even increase your problem-solving and decision-making skills. In fact, those who focus on their highest values before a stressful event show a substantial decrease in the stress hormone cortisol. When you focus on what you value, it puts all the stressors into perspective.

Clarifying your values is imperative to making the best choices in life—choices that take you down the path toward personal and professional fulfillment. Therefore, you need to be able to identify your values. And that's only the first step. Since your family and employees will believe what they see more than what you say, demonstrating your values is more important than talking about them. Believing that clarity is power, the following is an exercise I used to help make better value-based decisions and plans. These five steps will empower you to know your values, show your values, and grow your values:

Make a list of your values (minimum five). (Choose from the list in the Limiting/Liberating table or write your own). Spend time thinking about this. If you struggle, call to mind some memorable moments where you were happiest in your life. What value(s) were you living?

For each value, write your own personal definition—not a dictionary or Wikipedia' definition, but yours.

Think about five to ten things you have done, the people you've interacted with—those occasions when you *successfully* demonstrated your values. Write them down.

Now comes your deepest work. Write down when you either *failed* to live up to your core values or could have demonstrated more commitment. This step was the most challenging for me yet provided the greatest insights.

Post your values where you can see them every day and cultivate a deeper connection with them. Focus on the ones you desire. Change the ones that limit you.

Knowing, Showing, and Growing Your Values Model
© Dianna Kokoszka

Figure 9: The Knowing, Showing, and Growing Your Values Model enables you to ingrain your values deeper in your thought process.

Growth is an inside job, so I am still working on myself! And I trust you will too!

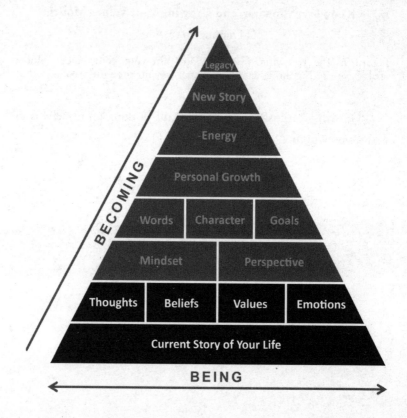

CHAPTER 10

EMOTIONS— FEELING THE FEELS

Your emotions are the slaves to your thoughts,
and you are the slave to your emotions.
—Elizabeth Gilbert

Have you ever wondered why some people can scale a towering rock face like in the movie *Free Solo*, while others cannot even watch from the comfort of their sofa without getting queasy?

Free solo rock climbing is done alone without ropes or protective equipment and is one of those sports that boggles the mind. One mistake could cost you your life. Alex Honnold is widely renowned for his extraordinary free solo feats, scaling some of the world's mightiest ascents.

Flying home from a speaking engagement, I had a chance to witness his skills by watching *Free Solo*, which documents his adventures climbing the three-thousand-foot El Capitan in Yosemite National Park. I couldn't believe what this man was capable of achieving. The photography depicted the precise and unique abilities Honnold possessed as he painstakingly navigated the mountain using the small cracks and indentations on the rocks and their edges to hold on. As he approached the summit, my whole body cringed when he appeared to come close to falling from the almost vertical slab of rock.

As the drama unfolded, I couldn't help but wonder what on earth was going on in his brain that allowed him to do what he does without fear, actually enjoying the challenge. I wasn't the only one watching intently. The lady in the seat next to me flinched each time Honnold released one hand and raised it up to grab hold of a nub on a rock that looked as if it could not even accommodate a small child's hand.

Suddenly I received a tap on the shoulder from my fellow traveler.

"Excuse me," she said so nicely. "Sorry I keep flinching; this movie has my insides in knots. I'm so sorry, I've worked to look away, yet I can't."

It was as though she wanted me to turn it off. It fascinated me how she had been drawn into my screen, sitting at the edge of her seat, and eventually interrupted me to express her discomfort. She helped me realize that some people could experience fear and anxiety just by watching, while others performing the task could feel exhilaration and triumph. I wondered if this movie would give us a clue as to how our emotions can be transformed into useful tools to allow us to become more.

There had to be a difference in the way their brains processed the same experience. Why else would one person do anything to avoid climbing free solo and another devote their life to experiencing it?

HOW WE PROCESS EXPERIENCES

Our past experiences affect how we confront new ones. According to Dr. Lisa Feldman Barrett of Northeastern University, emotions are not reactions to external events but are reactions to *concepts and stories* about the events that are constructed by our brain.[1] Some stories create happy emotions making you smile or laugh, while others create feelings of distress and fear. Our brain's amygdala regulates emotions and memories. When it's underactive, we feel less fear and perform better. The more it is activated, the more fear we experience.

In our brain, the thalamus sends sensory input to both the cortex and the amygdala simultaneously. The cortex is responsible for decision-making, while the amygdala helps generate an emotional response. Interestingly, the distance between the amygdala (emotional) and thalamus is shorter than between the cortex (decision-making) and the thalamus, meaning we experience emotion faster—before we can rationally assess it.

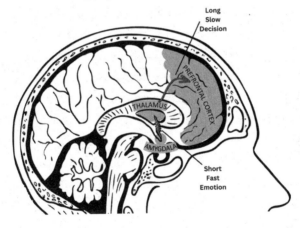

Emotional vs. Logical Decisions © Dianna Kokoszka

Figure 10: Emotional vs. Logical Decisions shows why people can act quickly with emotion over logic. You can visibly see the distance is shorter from the thalamus to the amygdala (emotional) than it is to the cortex (decision-making).

---

[1] Barrett, Lisa Feldman. *How Emotions Are Made: The Secret Life of the Brain.* HarperCollins, 2017.

As a result, many of us spend our days in a *ready-fire!-aim* mode, about to explode into an emotion before we have decided what is going on. Even the smallest stimulation can provoke a response that is much more emotional than logical.

The good news is that we can train ourselves to wait so that we're not just responding like loose cannons. When you wait, the cortex has time to *think*. I like to call this *ready-aim-aim-fire!* mode. Professional archers take a deep breath and then pull the arrow *back* before they aim and release. We can hit a bull's-eye when we fire with calm, rationality, and clear direction in the moment. Have you ever reacted instead of responding? I know I have, more than once!

How large is the gap between your stimulus and the response you give? If it's small, it generally bites you! Knowing this, we can put behind us our reactions and put in front of us our reflections. Reaction is pure emotion that happens immediately and subconsciously, while reflection is a more thoughtful and deliberate response that is logical in light of the emotion.

It might take some time to train yourself to not immediately respond to what you *feel,* to take a breath, wait, and measure the best response. The more you do this, the more your emotional intelligence (EQ) grows, which is more important for success than your IQ.

When emotions are involved, you live your life in one of two ways: as a thermometer or a thermostat. The thermometer has one job: to react to the environment in which it is placed. The thermostat is more advanced: it reads and reflects what the environment is and makes the environment react to it. You can be a thermometer, instantly reacting to your emotions and feelings, or a thermostat that reads the emotion, reflects on it, and adjusts for the appropriate action or response to follow.

EMOTIONS ARE NOT YOUR FEELINGS

Contrary to popular belief, feelings and emotions are not inter-changeable. They do, however, work together. The moment you attach a meaning to your emotions you create a feeling. We often confuse them because our feelings are conscious, while our emotions reside in the subconscious. This is why emotions sometimes gush out and surprise us.

EMOTIONS CONNECT THE BODY AND MIND

Another myth many people believe is that thought and emotion are *un*related. Thoughts are not just mental, and emotions are not just physical reactions to external stimuli. The truth is rather different. They flow to and from each other.

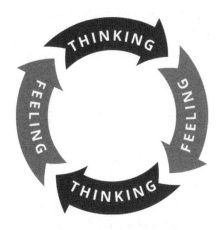

Mind–Body Cycle Model © Dianna Kokoszka

Figure 11: Thoughts evoke emotions; emotions direct the body's response. The body then gives feedback to the brain, which perpetuates thinking patterns.

When you think insecure thoughts, you take on feelings of insecurity. Feeling insecure causes you to have more insecure thoughts, and the cycle repeats over and over again. The mind–body connection pattern continues until there is a pattern interrupt, which is the cause of a new thought or new action resulting in a new emotion. This is much like telling an upset friend a joke; they may pause their anger or sadness long enough to laugh, and while they could go right back to an upset state, it will not be at the same intensity. The change of thought has interrupted the loop taking place from the mind (thinking) to the body (feeling). The combination of your thoughts and emotions leads to actions that move you up the ladder of success, or not.

Thoughts, beliefs, and values—all abstract, logical, or irrational—converge with your emotions to help you make decisions about what action you will take. Each decision provides an experience that, in turn, creates a memory that an emotion is attached to. Logic makes you think things through; emotion makes you act them out.

Following your emotions and ignoring the facts will limit you, just as following the facts and ignoring your emotions will frustrate you. It's not that you shouldn't have emotions. We all do—it proves we're human. The problem is how long you allow yourself to live in the emotion, sometimes reacting over and over again, and *in the same way*. Since feelings dominate, you must go from what you feel to what you do. Dr. Joe Dispenza teaches,

> If you allow that emotional reaction to last for hours or days, it's called a mood. If you keep that same emotional reaction for weeks or months, it's called a temperament. If you keep it for years, it's called a personality trait.

Our thoughts—positive or negative—activate the hypothalamus gland in our brain to release chemicals as they simultaneously signal emotions. These chemicals get stored in our cells, creating a chain reaction throughout the body. If this same thought is repeated, it will continue to stir up the same emotion releasing the same chemical, and over time, like the chemicals in alcohol or drugs, we can become addicted to the chemicals provided by our thoughts and emotions. We build up a tolerance, therefore needing more stimulus to satisfy us. This is why people can become more dramatic in their actions, making it more challenging to break their habitual ways but not impossible.

YOUR EMOTIONS ARE PART OF YOUR EVERYDAY LIFE

According to psychologists Paul Ekman and Wallace Friesen, there are six basic emotions: happiness, sadness, disgust, fear, surprise, and anger.[2] Each emotion is uniquely experienced and impacts our lives, shaping us into the individuals we are being at any moment.

It's no secret that there are two emotions affecting many people and the numbers seem to be on the rise: *anxiety and depression*. Have you ever thought about what might be behind the increase? A 2015 study published in the *Journal of Social and Clinical Psychology* made a significant contribution to the ongoing discussion surrounding the relationship between social media and depression by identifying a key factor that plays a crucial role: *social comparison*. The study found that the act of constantly comparing ourselves to others can lead to feelings of inadequacy and low self-esteem, and is a significant predictor of depression.

---

[2] Paul Ekman, "Basic Emotions," cited in T. Dalgleish and M. J. Power, *Handbook of Cognition and Emotion* (Hoboken, NJ: John Wiley & Sons, 1999), 45–57, https://onlinelibrary.wiley.com/doi/10.1002/0470013494.ch3.

Self-esteem is the difference between where you believe you are and where you think you should be compared to others.
—DANIEL G. AMEN, MD

EMOTIONS CAN BE TRIGGERED

Have you ever struggled to keep your emotions reeled in? You felt like you had stuffed them so far down they would never be seen? Then all of a sudden, out of nowhere, something happened, the floodgates opened, and all those emotions gushed out. You're shocked to find yourself feeling and expressing emotions you didn't even know you had!

What is it that triggers us?

We all have different needs, and when our needs are not being met, our emotions can flare up. Maybe we have a strong need to be in control, appreciated, respected, or a desire to be recognized. When that recognition is going elsewhere, we react.

Triggers are everywhere. Have you ever had a certain aroma bring back a happy memory? Has a certain event brought back memories of a past trauma? This is your hippocampus working, giving *meaning* and *significance* to an emotional experience. Your mind may not recall the exact facts of a past experience completely, yet it is incredibly accurate in recalling the emotions you felt.

This demonstrates how our mind is often inaccurate in interpreting a current circumstance. By knowing what triggers us, we can "retrain" our mind—give it new neural pathways—so that past emotional experiences don't dictate how we view our present or our future. Using your emotions as data to help you think differently will help you live longer and healthier—and become more.

SURRENDER

Negative emotions can be uncomfortable, but they are telling us something. They serve as valuable indicators that an area in our life needs attention. However, it's essential to remember that sharing negative emotions, such as anger, with others may not always be the best course of action. When they agree with us, the emotion escalates and intensifies, like adding fuel to the fire already raging. It's best to find healthy and appropriate ways to process and cope with these emotions. Want to calm down? Call a calm person, exercise, or hit a pillow!

According to Jeffrey Nevid in his *Psychology Today* blog emotions are triggered by thoughts that in turn are strengthened by the emotions themselves. In the case of negative emotions such as anger, it may start with an angry thought, but to sustain the anger, you must keep focusing on the object of your anger (someone or something). Just thinking of being angry without someone or something to direct it to makes it fade away. The quickest way to end anger is to surrender to it, let go of the person or event that caused it, and practice forgiveness.[3]

Have you ever seen a Chinese finger trap? It is a simple woven bamboo tube into which you insert your index fingers, one into each end of the contraption. When you work to pull your fingers out, the mesh tube constricts, trapping your fingers.

When I was introduced to one of these, I kept focusing on escaping, pulling and tugging, making the trap grow tighter and tighter until finally it broke. The trap symbolizes our emotions and the consequences we may experience based on how we utilize them.

---

[3] Jeffrey S. Nevid, "Feeling Your Thoughts: Are Emotions and Thoughts Really as Separate as People May Think?" *Psychology Today*, December 23, 2015, https://www.psychologytoday.com/us/blog/the-minute-therapist/201512/feeling-your-thoughts.

Resisting them or arguing with them is not the answer. As Carl Jung said, "What we resist, persists."

What I discovered was if instead of struggling against the trap I did the reverse—pushing my fingers inward—it caused the mesh to loosen and created some wiggle room. Using my thumbs, I was able to ease my fingers out of the trap. The art lies in surrendering to the emotion, at least for the moment, thereby allowing a new perspective to emerge and free us from it.

EMOTIONS ARE A CHOICE

Some people blame someone else for feeling upset, insecure, or envious. Believe me, no one has that kind of power over another. We choose the emotion or feeling we will have based on the story we make up in our mind. And although you must own them, *you are not your emotions*. In Ireland people say, *"ta bron orm"* when they feel sad. Literally translated, this means "there is sadness on me," not "I am sad." This is a wonderful saying that prevents you from accepting sadness as part of your identity.

Using words such as *I feel* upset instead of I *am* upset, or *I feel* angry instead of *you made me* angry helps us distinguish this. Since we are the only ones who make ourselves feel a certain way, the honest way to express this is, "I am *choosing* to feel upset." Then you are giving yourself permission to choose to think differently, allowing a new feeling to emerge. In this way, past pains become learning experiences that you don't have to experience anymore.

Have you ever observed someone not moving beyond those past pains? During a leadership program I had written and was teaching in California, it came time for an exercise to transform emotions. Everyone in the class agreed to be called on at any time. When Ashley Lunn's name was chosen, I was thrilled.

Here is how she described it later:

As was typical for me at that time, I doubted if I was qualified to be in the room, working to be invisible, wondering why I had agreed to be vulnerable. There I was with forty other leaders—all people I felt subordinate and inferior to.

Dianna was introducing a new demonstration. I remember very clearly putting my head down and reading my notes silently chanting, "Don't call on me." Dianna called out a number that corresponded to the name of a registered attendee. The adrenaline that flushed my system when she called my number made it nearly impossible to stand.

As I walked up to the "stage" I felt exposed, vulnerable, and terrified. Little did I know that the demonstration Dianna was going to take me through would alter everything, especially my emotions, for the better.

What Dianna taught she called Context/Resource. She had me stand on a paper labeled Context and describe something in my personal life or business that was limiting me. At the time, the growth of our business was stunted because I was not willing to call people I didn't know and speak with them about our business. Dianna had me explain how I felt when making those calls, describing my fear in detail. Then she asked for more detail. And more. Until I felt completely naked in front of my colleagues.

During that experience, she literally held me up with her

hand, steadying my shaking. She pulled the full Context of my fear out of me. Next, she had me step off the Context label and distracted me with some witty remarks. Then she had me step forward to another paper, this one labeled Resource. And she asked me of a time when I felt powerful, strong, invincible, and joyful. It took me a few moments before I described being on the starting line of a road race, knowing I was going to dominate the other runners.

She again asked for more detail, getting me to describe not only the feelings but also to feel them as if I were in that race right then. I felt more confident, powerful, and in control. With my eyes closed I was able to see myself as a powerful person, instead of the vulnerable and powerless person I had gone into this exercise as.

After the description and experience of my Resource, she once again broke the pattern of my thinking and we continued to go back and forth—Context, Resource—describing the same events over and over until it was as though she had connected the dots and knew intuitively, I had my power. Somehow, she had lifted me to where I visualized and felt the emotions putting me in my most powerful state of mind, transferring those emotions to what I feared. She taught me that at any time I could resurrect and apply those confident, powerful thoughts and emotions to whatever I was facing. That exercise and teaching transformed everything for me.

Walking off that stage, I felt I belonged in that room and was in fact a leader among leaders. From that moment on, I was able to harness the confidence, belief, and power needed for every challenging situation I have faced. Now, as soon as I feel the desire to avoid something, I am triggered and I run toward it. I use the Resource that Dianna pulled out of me to power up. What she taught me in that twenty-minute exercise has allowed me to build strong businesses, counsel people and couples through the topics most avoid, confront behavioral issues most ignore, successfully navigate tough legal situations, and most recently address the end-of-life conversations and decisions no one wants to make. In all these situations, and many more, I use Context/Resource to tackle my toughest challenges.

I love that! As Ashley's story illustrates, both *context* and *resource* are emotional experiences of the past. Her limiting emotional experience served as the context, whereas the emotions of success and achievement were the resource. She discovered that by resourcing the emotions of success she could exchange the limiting emotions of context.

Where did the emotions Ashley felt before and after the exercise come from? From herself. She went from the limiting power of fear to the liberating power of courage. And so can you!

LIMITING AND LIBERATING EMOTIONS

In a scene in the movie *Three Kings*, Archie Gates (portrayed by George Clooney) is caught in a battle among soldiers. Another character asks him why he has so much courage.

"The way it works is, you do the thing you're scared of, and you get the courage *after* you do it, not before you do it!" he replies.

That is so true. Fear is often transformed into courage by *stepping out*. Fear is one of the most powerful, primitive emotions all of us experience. It is also one that limits us as much, or more, as any other single emotion. By surrendering fear and substituting it with faith and courage, we change our world.

Another limiting emotion is envy. The most challenging thing about envy is it is never satisfied.

> *When you get what you envy,*
> *there's something else to envy.*
> *It will always be at work*
> *finding other things.*
> —DR. HENRY CLOUD

Two emotions we can zero in on that will help bring meaning to our lives are *love* and *forgiveness*. Many times, these emotions take effort when someone has wronged us. This is why they are liberating. We breathe easier when we love and forgive others.

Knowing our emotions are unique to us and impact our lives in powerful ways, it is imperative to be intentional about transforming them from limiting to liberating. Consider the differences between those two qualities among the following emotions:

Limiting vs. Liberating Emotions

Limiting Emotions	Liberating Emotions
Outrage	Forgiveness
Fear	Faith/Courage
Jealousy/Envy	Commitment/Gratitude
Anxiety	Passion
Guilt	Love
Apprehension	Inspiration

When you experience any of the limiting emotions in the left column, complete the following exercise and watch them transform.

Let's take anxiety, for example: When things are unfamiliar or uncertain, causing a lack of control, anxiety can set in. Completing these steps may help your limiting anxiety to fade away, turning instead to liberating passion.

- Make a list of things you cannot control in your life that are causing you anxiety (the more items the better).

- Set a timer for ten minutes. Stare at the list and focus on the items. Allow yourself to complain in private about each one.

- When the buzzer goes off, rip up the paper and throw it away.

- Now write down the things you are passionate about and focus on those throughout the day.

- Repeat this every morning until your list shrinks as anxiety ceases to come to mind.

The chapters you have just worked through, from Thoughts to Emotions, complete the foundation you are building on your journey to *becoming more*. Many more discoveries and life changes await. Let's continue . . .

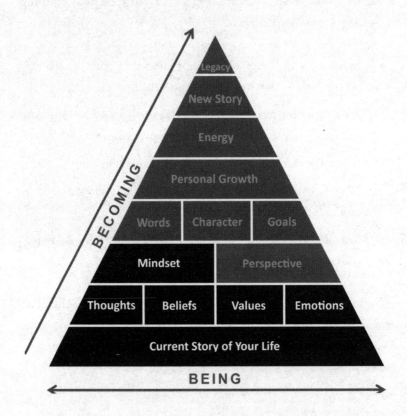

CHAPTER 11

MINDSET 1— DYNAMICS

*The opponent within one's own head is
more formidable than the one
on the other side of the net.*
—Timothy Galloway

C ollege was upon me. I thought I'd be attending the University
of Utah, where I was awarded a partial academic scholarship.
Instead, I moved to Denver with my parents. We were facing hardships as a family, so the decision was made for me to live at home. I
found myself working three jobs, attending school, and wondering
every day, *Why am I here?* It made no sense at the time. Of course,
now, upon reflection, I know the experience prepared me for the
opportunities ahead.

I worked in telemarketing, selling home care products door-
to-door, as a hostess at a Holiday Inn, and later in a physics lab.
These jobs were just about as varied and different from one another
as they might sound! Yet through them, I discovered the dedicated
study and skill-building required of a salesperson, the importance
of continued progress in service roles, and the ways in which the

principles of energy affect our daily lives. Talk about an out-of-classroom education!

Years later, a real estate agent named Rosanna began reaching out to me persistently. She'd sold us our first home and now wanted to sell me on an idea. "You are a great salesperson!" she insisted. "After all, you managed to pay your college tuition by selling home care products at a mere 90 cents per bottle. Plus, your love for people shines through. You should pursue a career in real estate where you can earn a substantial income with each transaction."

Her encouragement stuck with me as I thought and dreamed on this idea.

One night, my child fell ill. But no matter how loud he cried, I found myself dozing off. Determined to stay awake, I turned on the television. As fate would have it, I ended up watching an auction aimed at raising funds for public television. And then, it happened: music to my ears! A real estate course went up for auction.

With the auctioneer's guidance on how to place a bid, I grabbed my checkbook, looked inside, and quickly calculated how much I could afford to bid. (Yes, it was one of those rare moments I let my checkbook do the thinking for me!) I knew I could spare $50 and still make ends meet. Immediately I thought, *Oh, Lord, really? A $1,000-plus class and I'm going to bid $50?* Just as quickly, another thought entered my mind. It was the voice of my parents saying, "Nothing ventured, nothing gained." So I went for it!

Taking a leap of faith, fully aware I may look foolish, I bid. Then I waited and watched as the bids closed. To my astonishment, I won! I was going to real estate school!

The following day reality set in. I had to face the facts: I couldn't afford a babysitter and had no family close by to rely on. I began to question my sanity, blaming the rash purchase on late-night exhaustion. Of course, I didn't want my $50 to go to waste, so off to school I went.

Five classes into my ten-class course, a major setback occurred. The instructor quit! We were given two options: wait for a new instructor or pay full tuition to attend another school.

It had been a gamble up to this point, so why not take another chance of betting on myself? Mustering up courage, I called with an unconventional proposal. I convinced the state to allow me to take the test that month, without completing the course—an opportunity that wouldn't even be available today. And guess what? I passed. License in hand, I had to figure out my next step.

I had two children not yet in school and I hoped to enter a field dominated by men (as it was in those days). How could I ever be the hero of my own story under those circumstances?

I especially felt the weight of this challenge as I went from one real estate office to another only to be told, "We already have a woman Realtor." Some even offered me a secretarial position instead! You can probably imagine how this fueled the fire within me. I was more determined than ever to find a secure place to establish myself as a licensed professional.

Twelve offices later, I finally found someone who uttered those magic words, "Yes, you can join us." They were willing to give me an opportunity. And in that moment, they earned my loyalty.

My parents raised me to believe that the only obstacles I faced were those in my own mind. Fighting first for my license and then for a job, I discovered my parents were right. My mindset is what got me through. It was and is one of the biggest contributors of my success and the success of others. We have to live *within* even if we are living *without*—to think of abundance and prosperity before it arrives.

And so, with my kids in a little red Radio Flyer wagon, I walked through the neighborhoods, knocking on doors, engaging in conversations, and convincing people to choose me as their Realtor. Day after day we ventured out, meeting people and asking for business. The average agent at the time sold five homes per year. To my surprise, I ended up helping 104 families buy or sell a home during my first twelve months. I felt more grateful and motivated than ever before!

From that year on, my career in real estate took a wild ride. I worked with individuals to buy and sell homes, wrote training courses, and managed offices, ultimately owning my own real estate company with four locations. There was a time when I thought I might lose everything. Perseverance and grit kept me working hard and pulled me through. Eventually, I became the CEO of a coaching and training company with the privilege and honor of leading a great team, growing it into the largest real estate coaching company in the world. I served as CEO for thirteen years before stepping down. And through it all I can say with confidence that what you believe about yourself is what you become. It really does all boil down to your mindset.

The road to success is not smooth. It will be riddled with potholes, curves, detours, and speed bumps. Just like life. I certainly didn't travel from success to success. It was more from failure to failure. There were days when I felt physically and mentally exhausted, when the price seemed too high—especially for my kids. Yet I learned that you must be willing to go through failure in order to get to success. And just when you think you've arrived, there are often more obstacles to push through. Perseverance is absolutely key. Challenges come along to strengthen you, to encourage you to become more. Let your mindset be a simple one: *Just get up and get going!*

Your mindset is a culmination of your thoughts, your beliefs, your values, and your emotions. Mindset comes in to play *precisely* in the moments where we make a choice. Do we see ourselves as the helpless victim, as pawns in a game bigger than us and completely outside of our control? Or do we see ourselves as heroes and over-comers, refusing to be determined or defined by our not-so-great moments? Our mindset is revealed not by what happens to us but by how we choose to *see* and then *respond*.

HOW POWERFUL IS OUR MINDSET?

This question is the subject of extensive research. In one study, researcher Fabrizio Benedetti observed a group of patients under-going thoracic surgery, which is exceptionally invasive and painful. For the research, Benedetti and his colleagues arranged for half of the patients to receive the required dose of morphine by a doctor at the bedside, while the other received an identical dose through IV by a preprogrammed pump.

You might think both groups would experience the same relief from pain. After all, the dosage amounts were identical. On the contrary, Fabrizio found that those who received the morphine directly from the doctor experienced significant reductions in pain compared to those who did not.

Researchers also used the same procedure, with different medi-cations, to test the effectiveness of treatments for anxiety, Parkinson's disease, and hypertension. The results consistently showed that those who expected to receive the benefits of the medication enjoyed effec-tive treatment, while those who were unaware of the medication did not enjoy similar benefits—even though all the groups received the same dosage of medicine!

Carol S. Dweck, a Stanford psychology professor, is a leader in the field of mindset research. In one study, she discovered that parents who praise children for fixed traits with phrases such as "You're so smart!"

or "You're the best!" or even "You're beautiful!" inadvertently enable their children to develop a fixed, limiting mindset.[1] Why? Because those words send the message that the child is either good or bad by *nature* and can do nothing to change. With this mindset, the child loses the desire to strive for better, causing them to fixate on a born identity rather than on who they are *becoming*. Eventually, these children will seek validation from others to prove they are what they've been told.

This doesn't mean we shouldn't praise our children. Goodness knows, we probably all believe our kids are smart and beautiful and capable of achieving greatness. The important thing to consider is how we go about the process of praising them. When we focus on praising effort instead of existence, we emphasize our child's potential as well as the power of perseverance. This sense of control fosters a liberating growth mindset and a belief that everyone can improve over time with work. Children with a fixed mindset see mistakes as failures. Children with a growth mindset see mistakes as learning opportunities.

Another study by David Scott Yeager and Geoffrey L. Cohen, professors of psychology at the University of Texas and Stanford University, respectively, took a look at the relationship between students and their teachers regarding expectations. The study found that students often strive to meet the expectations set by a teacher with high standards who also shows a belief in the students' ability to *reach* those standards.[2] Providing clear objectives from the start and offering constructive feedback creates a sense of belonging and fosters a growth mindset.

---

[1] Carole S. Dweck, cited in Clifton B. Parker, "Perseverance Key to Children's Intellectual Growth, Stanford Scholar Says," *Stanford News*, April 29, 2015, https://news.stanford .edu/2015/04/29/dweck-kids-potential-042915/.

[2] David S. Yeager et al., "Breaking the Cycle of Mistrust: Wise Interventions to Provide Critical Feedback across the Racial Divide," *Journal of Experiential Psychology* 2014, Vol. 143, no. 2 (2014): 804–24, https://www.apa.org/pubs/journals/releases/xge-a0033906.pdf.

In one of my favorite ads Michael Jordan did for Nike, he said, "I've missed more than nine thousand shots. I've lost almost three hundred games. Twenty-six times, I've been trusted to take the game-winning shot and missed." I love this vulnerability from Jordan. I also appreciate that he committed to practicing the shots he missed—constantly improving so the next time he found himself in the same situation, he would be more prepared to succeed.

Our mindset acts as a powerful force in our lives. It would be rather tragic to think of the mind as fixed and unchangeable, like the color of our eyes or hair (although even these can be artificially altered). The good news? Mindsets *can* be changed.

MINDSET VS. ATTITUDE

Many of us were told as children to keep a positive attitude. Yet were you ever told to have a positive *mindset?* What kind of difference might this one word make? Think about it like this: When we hire someone in the business world, we often ask, "What is their attitude like?" Yet when we talk about an athlete, we often discuss whether or not they have a "winning *mindset.*" Why?

As we've seen, mindset wins out over attitude every single time. Confuse these and you'll struggle to liberate your mindset. Here are a few of the key differences.

Attitude vs. Mindset

Attitude	Mindset
Can be adjusted in real time	Will show up automatically
Conscious choice	Subconscious
Can be faked	Can self-sabotage you (without you even realizing)
Can change in a moment	Takes constant and consistent effort to change
Has little to do with the circumstances you are in	Affects your decisions, which affects the circumstances you are in

Remember: mindset refers to the totality of how you think and evaluate the world based on your experiences, thoughts, beliefs, values, and emotions. Attitude simply refers to how you interact with the world based on your current mood.

Imagine a problem arises and you're upset. If you have a judgmental mindset, you may quickly form an opinion. On the other hand, if you have a positive attitude even with a judgmental mindset, you will express yourself in a more thoughtful way. When you adopt a curious (nonjudgmental) mindset, you are more likely to ask questions to understand what happened. Your attitude will determine the type of questions you'll ask. Mindset drives actions, attitude executes them.

According to mindset and leadership coach Cheryl Himburg, attitude comes from our conscious mind and is responsible for only 5 percent of our thinking and actions. Meanwhile, our mindset—found in the subconscious—makes up the remaining 95 percent. Reflecting on this, it stands to reason that we should work to change our mindset so we can be swiftly propelled toward victory.

THE MINDSET OF THE SUCCESSFUL

If you go through history and find the athletes, the heroes, the pioneers, the entrepreneurs; the people who beat the odds and silenced the critics; those who did what the naysayers said could not be done—in every field—what will you find most have in common? Successful people possess a growth mindset. They know the past is gone, the future is inaccessible, and choices happen in the present. They believe skills are important and can be grown. They live in the *now*, yet they are not content with the *now*. *Successful people* constantly work to wrestle the *not yet* into being.

The movie *Moneyball* does a wonderful job depicting what happens when we allow the past a foothold in the present. Jeremy

Brown—a 240-pound catcher for the Oakland A's—struggled with confidence when it came to running the bases. He worried about his speed and never attempted a double, even when he got a good hit. On one occasion, though, Jeremy got hold of a fastball and sent it deep and high down the middle of the field.

For some reason, he decides to do something new: go for the double. He rounds first and heads toward second, when all of a sudden, his mindset of negativity and doubt takes over. He's thrown right back into the past where all his worst nightmares live. And in the present, Jeremy slips and falls. He scrambles back up, hugging first base tightly, as everyone in the stands—and many in the dugout—laugh.

Of course, we learn that Jeremy's fans and teammates aren't laughing because of his fumble. They're aware of a truth that Jeremy doesn't yet see: He hit a home run—with the ball flying sixty feet over the fence! So ingrained was his mindset of negativity and doubt that all he could think about was hanging on to first base and playing it safe. How many home runs have you hit without giving yourself credit? How many victories have you experienced and not acknowledged? How many compliments do you receive with a shrug and do not accept them? People with a fixed mindset believe nothing can change—that their health, intelligence, and skills are predetermined and locked in. People with a growth mindset, however, see the potential in themselves and others. They firmly believe they can improve in almost anything—be it athletics, mathematics, or even artistic ability. As Dweck explains, "Everyone can change and grow through application and experience."[3]

---

[3] Carol S. Dweck, *Mindset: The New Psychology of Success* (New York: Ballantine, 2007), Kindle Location 154.

SHIFTING YOUR MINDSET

You probably recognize the term *choking under pressure*. This refers to the moment when an athlete recognizes that success is close—so close they can nearly reach out to grasp it—only to find it slipping through their fingers.

Texas Longhorns football coach Mack Brown is well known for leading his team to a seminal victory at the 2006 Rose Bowl against USC—the Longhorns' first national championship in thirty-four years. Sitting in his hotel room prior to the game, he watched as every channel on TV declared that Texas would surely be slaughtered, trampled, and mutilated by USC. He could find no reprieve as he flipped the channels.

Eventually, Brown landed on *The Jerry Springer Show*. This show was new to him, and he didn't care for it. Of course, Jerry wasn't talking about football, so Mack let go of the remote and watched for over an hour—anything to get his mind off the negative publicity.

For two days prior, Brown wondered what he might say before the game to help his team to relax. He knew they could get caught up in the fact that people did not believe they'd win. He was adamant about the boys going out on the field with the right mindset so they could play the game to their highest ability and have fun doing it.

Game day arrived and he knew what he would say. There in the locker room Coach Brown asked his team, "How many of you have watched *The Jerry Springer Show*?"

Almost every hand went up. He was shocked they even knew it existed.

"I'm going to tell you something that's going to change your life, and it's going to help us win this football game."

The team went silent with anticipation.

He looked around and then said, "If your girlfriend or your wife ever asks you to be on *The Jerry Springer Show*, don't go! It's not going to be good for you!"

The players broke out into laughter.

"That's right!" Brown said. "Let's have some fun. We're not gonna work this hard and lay an egg! We're not gonna go out there uptight!"

The team went out ready to play, and play they did! After the game Coach Brown congratulated them for the win and once again seemed to have the right words. "Do not let this victory become the biggest defining moment in your life. Find other things to define you. Become a great father, great businessman, great husband!"

This story illustrates that mindset shifts don't always need to be serious and drastic. A brief change in your mindset—even a silly one!—can go a long way toward resetting your focus on what matters most on your journey toward becoming more. Imagine the results after making consistent long-lasting changes to your mindset!

According to research from Yale epidemiologist Becca Levy, when we are able to see aging not as a deterioration of our bodies but rather as a positive process of gaining wisdom and growth, we will not only lead healthier lives we may also extend the length of our lives as well. That's the power of a positive mindset.

Let's also take a look at the research on stress. Studies consistently show that perceiving stress as a *catalyst* for peak performance leads to an enhanced work experience characterized by positive outcomes. That's precisely why—as explained by psychology professor Dr. Alia Crum—the most remarkable sports plays happen in the most intense moments.[4] So shifting your mindset is not only possible; it is preferable.

---

[4] Alia Crum, "Change Your Mindset, Change the Game," TEDxTraverseCity, October 15, 2014, https://www.youtube.com/watch?v=0tqq66zwa7g.

LIMITING VS. LIBERATING MINDSET

If you were to search for *mindset* on Google, you would find a wide range of examples that may not be relevant in our everyday thinking. After extensive study, I have identified what I believe are the most essential mindsets to unlock your potential.

Physics acknowledges the law of duality, where distinct elements converge to make a unified whole. Like the way a rainbow appears when water droplets, air, and light intertwine, our mindset consists of a blend of various limiting and liberating factors that coexist within us. It's not a matter of simply replacing a limiting mindset, for both always exist. The goal is to intentionally focus on which one you desire to cultivate and nurture.

Limiting vs. Liberating Mindsets

Limiting Mindsets	Liberating Mindsets
Fixed	Growth
Entitlement	Gratitude
Doubt	Confident
Scarcity	Abundant
Negative	Positive
Hubris	Humility
Judgment	Curiosity

By completing the assessment (becomingmorebook.com) you will be introduced to the possibilities of which limiting and liberating mindset you choose to nurture.

It's crucial to recognize the role of choice in shaping your mindset. The degree to which your mindset is liberating or limiting is directly influenced by the decisions you make or neglect to make each day. Changing your mindset is so significant that we will spend the next chapter unpacking our mindset and empowering you with the critical tools you need for your journey to becoming more.

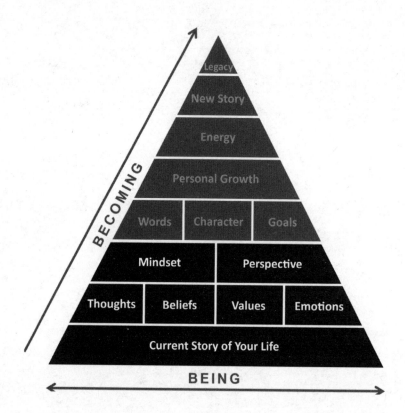

CHAPTER 12

MINDSET 2— LIBERATION

To change your life, you must change your mindset.
—Brad Turnbull

As we discussed in the previous chapter, the mindset you adopt will profoundly influence how you navigate life. A limiting mindset constrains you with the illusion of fears and self-imposed restrictions. It directs your attention toward obstacles and challenges. It's no wonder a person with a limiting mindset will hesitate to take risks or embrace new experiences.

On the other hand, a liberating mindset focuses on *possibilities*. With this mindset, you firmly believe in your ability to expand your talents through effort and commitment. Consequently, you are more prone to step outside your comfort zone as you move toward success.

Let's take a closer look at the eight categories of limiting versus liberating mindsets that we first discussed in the previous chapter. We'll talk through the characteristics of each one as well as offer encouragement for navigating those pivotal decision points in your efforts to change.

To gain insights on your own existing mindsets, you

may also consider taking the Learn Your Mindset assessment at becomingmorebook.com.

Are you ready? Here we go.

The Eight Categories of Limiting Mindsets vs. Liberating Mindsets

FIXED VS. GROWTH MINDSET

> *A fixed mindset is the lock*
> *on the door to opportunity.*
> —CAROL S. DWECK

Fixed Mindset: You believe that character, intelligence, and creativity are predetermined and cannot be substantially altered regardless of effort. People with this mindset are resistant to feedback because they believe they already possess all the necessary answers, or they lack the intelligence to learn since everyone's IQ is fixed and cannot be altered. Looking good and being right are essential to their existence.

> *The growth mindset allows people*
> *to value what they are doing*
> *regardless of the outcome.*
> —CAROL S. DWECK

Growth Mindset: You believe abilities and intelligence can be developed through dedication and focused work. You're open to new ideas and constantly seek out opportunities to learn and improve. Resilient in embracing challenges, you keep going until you've successfully completed a task. You welcome criticism and feedback as valuable opportunities for growth and genuinely celebrate the success of others.

Decision Point: Transitioning from a fixed mindset to a growth mindset can be challenging yet possible with practice. To help you on your journey, make a point to do the following:

- Embrace challenges and failures, viewing them as an opportunity to learn.

- Acknowledge that making mistakes is a natural part of the learning process.

- Focus on the knowledge you're gaining and be sure to celebrate your effort and progress.

- Commit to learning from great thought leaders through books, podcasts, seminars, and more.

- Seek honest, constructive feedback and see it as an opportunity to improve.[1]

ENTITLEMENT VS. GRATITUDE MINDSET

*Entitlement is a delusion
built on self-centeredness and laziness.*
—UNKNOWN

Entitlement: You believe you deserve things you have not worked

---

[1] Carol S. Dweck coined these terms in *Mindset*, 2007.

for. They should be given to you because you are you. You may find yourself blaming others for whatever goes wrong in your life because taking responsibility is not part of this mindset. Entitlement rarely finds you showing respect to all those who helped you open doors or paved a path for advancement.

> *It's not joy that makes us grateful;*
> *it is gratitude that makes us joyful.*
> —DAVID STEINDL-RAST

Gratitude: You're appreciative for all you have while pursuing more, never complaining about what you don't have.

Embracing gratitude leads to a more positive and abundant mindset, as it's impossible to be both grateful and negative at the same time. Plus, grateful people experience the benefits of enhanced creativity, increased physical and emotional well-being, stronger relationships, less stress, and more compassion. My daughter-in-law, Rosy, along with my grandsons Armando and Dante made me a beautiful gratitude box that sits on my dresser. Inside they placed a small pencil and several papers with the saying, "I am grateful for . . ." Each day I write down five things I'm grateful for. This simple practice changes the outlook of my day—every single day.

Decision Point: To start cultivating gratitude, practice the following:

- Focus on what you have, not what you lack.

- Recognize and appreciate all the people who have helped you, for no one succeeds alone.

- Look for ways to add value to others daily.

- Congratulate and encourage others in their progress toward success.

- Engage in volunteer work or activities that provide service to others.

- Write notes or make calls to people for whom you are grateful.

- Recognize that everything you have is a gift.

Another idea: take a gratitude walk. As you stroll through your neighborhood or the park, reflect on the things you are thankful for. On your way back, or halfway through your walk, express gratitude or think of ways to demonstrate appreciation for everything you thought of as well as other things that come to mind. This can include simple things such as the convenience of hot water during your morning shower, the ability to pay your bills, people who have helped you, or even the gift of good health. Additionally, you can practice giving "gratitude in advance" for things you desire and don't yet have. This positive energy aids to bring those desires into reality.

As a leader, I started our daily stand-up meetings with gratitude. Each employee would write three things they were grateful for on a piece of paper and place the paper in a large gratitude basket. When guests visited the office, they would often comment on the energy in the room. I knew the mindset of gratitude was not only keeping us positive but also adding to the bottom line, for the profits continued to increase.

DOUBT VS. CONFIDENCE MINDSET

Doubt yourself and
you doubt everything.
—NANCY LOPEZ

Doubt: You question everything—big decisions and small decisions—and you rely on others to fill in the gaps. When your mind is uncertain, caught between two or more conflicting points of view, you don't trust yourself. It is like being in checkmate, with nowhere to move.

> *You have to have confidence in your ability,*
> *and then be tough enough to follow through.*
> —ROSALYNN CARTER

Confidence: You know who you are—always moving forward with assurance because you are not defined by success or failure.

Having a confident mindset doesn't equate to having an oversized ego. A confident person doesn't parade around as though they have all the answers. True confidence comes from knowing you are capable of accomplishing something without seeking external validation. It means continuing to move forward, even when mistakes are made. Confidence in yourself brings staying power and creativity. And creativity helps bring forth an answer.

Decision Point: To move toward a mindset of confidence, focus on these actions:

- Identify and challenge your negative self-talk. Say positive affirmations that counteract those thoughts.

- Focus on your strengths and past successes.

- Take small steps outside of your comfort zone to experience new things. Each small success will boost your confidence and motivate you to take on bigger challenges.

- Keep a "victory log" of things you accomplish and the things that give you a sense of accomplishment. When doubt creeps in—and it will from time to time—grab your victory log and read it to remind yourself of all you are and all you are becoming.

- Don't compare yourself to other people, especially on social media.

- Avoid negative or critical people who bring you down and contribute to self-doubt.

- Borrow others' beliefs in you—people who encourage and inspire you.

Having confidence in your ability to become more today goes a long way toward expanding your idea of what is possible. And the great thing about confidence is that it can be cultivated, one small success at a time, as the doubt gradually fades away.

SCARCITY VS. ABUNDANCE MINDSET

> *There is no scarcity of opportunity to make a living at what you love; there's only scarcity of resolve to make it happen.*
> —Wayne Dyer

Scarcity: Scarcity is like looking at life through a keyhole, limiting your vision of possibilities. You live with the notion that there isn't enough money, time, or opportunity. Those with this mindset may experience feelings of inadequacy and constantly harbor fears, viewing their world with limited resources. Competing and fighting for what you desire is commonplace since resources and opportunities are limited. You are often driven by a sense of fear, insecurity, and a feeling of lack. You tend to focus on what you don't have or what you might lose.

The key to abundance is meeting limited circumstances with unlimited thoughts.
—MARIANNE WILLIAMSON

Abundance: You have a firm belief that there is plenty for everyone, with more continually being produced. Opportunities are accessible for everybody. Generosity is an inherent aspect of your life—always willing to give of your knowledge, time, and/or money. You believe the world is infinite and everyone can enjoy it!

If you believe in an abundant universe, then you are free from the pettiness and small-mindedness that can get in the way of growth and achievement. Celebrating the victories of others without feeling threatened comes naturally. You enjoy encouraging others and building them up with sincerity. When someone takes a slice of pie, you know that doesn't leave you with less because the pie isn't finite; there is always a baker making more. Life becomes less of a competition and more of a cooperation—like we witness when athletes help one another over the finish line.

Decision Point: Here are some steps that can help you shift from a mindset of scarcity to abundance:

- Reframe your thoughts by looking around and noticing all the abundance that surrounds you. After all, you cannot count the number of leaves on a tree in the summertime, the grains of sand on the beach, or the blades of grass on a lawn.

- Realize opportunities are abundant; they're never lost, just found by someone else. Stay abundant-minded by learning from experience and seize the next opportunity.

- When you see something in a store that you like and the price is higher than you can afford, say "I can't afford it *yet!*" Train your brain to know that in the future there will be a time you can buy it if you desire.

- Read articles and books to gain new insights on money and wealth.

- Interview people you admire for their abundance mindset, asking questions around their thoughts and perspectives more than just techniques, as the same actions with the wrong mindset will not produce the same results.

- Make a "dream board" of things you aspire to be, do, have, or give. This could be a family project with pictures you find on the Internet or in magazines placed in a dream book or on a poster or corkboard.

NEGATIVE VS. POSITIVE MINDSET

A negative mind will
never give a positive life.
—ZIAD K. ABDELNOUR

Negative: A negative mindset is characterized by a pessimistic outlook, focused on what is wrong versus what is right, finding the bad aspects of any situation. Many times, a negative mindset has you believing bad things will happen to you, which in turn produces fear or anxiety that can debilitate you and keep you from becoming more.

*Optimism is a
happiness magnet.*
—MARY LOU RETTON

Positive: Having a positive mindset doesn't mean you think things will always be OK; it means you will be OK regardless of the outcome.

Much research has shown that having a positive mindset has a big impact on your mental and physical health. This doesn't mean that you ignore reality or make light of problems. It does, however, mean you know how to see things from a broader perspective.

Decision Point: How do we go from a negative to a positive mindset?

- Reframe your negative thoughts by focusing on what could go *right*.

- Write positive affirmations and say them daily. Remember to write them in the present tense such as, "I am a person who sees the good in all people and in all things."

- Choose a mantra such as my personal one: "Things are always working out for me." So no matter what happens, you can remain in an open, positive state.

- Seek positive environments.

- Set goals and take action toward them. Even if it is a small step, you will feel more positive.

- When things don't work out as planned, don't be too hard on yourself. Learn and quickly look for other ways to obtain the results desired.

HUBRIS VS. HUMILITY MINDSET

> *Hubris blinds us to our*
> *weaknesses and blocks*
> *our path to growth.*
>
> —UNKNOWN

Hubris: Having exaggerated pride in yourself, your abilities, and your importance in the world. Hubris develops when you start believing your own press, thinking your accomplishments were only of your own doing. It leads us to believe we can control everything. Of course, all it takes is a natural disaster to remind us of our limitations.

> *Humility is not thinking*
> *less of yourself, it is thinking*
> *of yourself less.*
>
> —RICK WARREN

Humility: This mindset centers on knowing your strengths and weaknesses—and not confusing them. The Greeks used the word *praus*, which meant "strength under control." Humility is just that—keeping your strengths under control, realizing that you are not doing everything yourself.

Decision Point: To move from hubris to humility, the following will help:

- Recognize your limitations and weaknesses, for no one is perfect. Everyone has strengths. And the inverse is also true:

everyone has weaknesses.

- Actively listen to others. Be interested in what they have to say.

- Embrace constructive feedback from others.

- Cultivate empathy by putting yourself in others' shoes as you consider their perspectives, acknowledging how your actions and words affect them.

- Be aware of others around you, taking the focus off yourself. Bottom line: get over yourself, for we all have room to grow.

- Encourage others; congratulate them on their accomplishments.

- Always show respect to others.

JUDGMENT VS. CURIOSITY MINDSET

> *When you judge someone else,*
> *you don't define them,*
> *you define yourself.*
> —EARL NIGHTINGALE

Judgment: People with this mindset quickly form (and express) opinions on everything without consideration of another's point of view. They're always willing to tell others where they have gone wrong or missed the mark.

They tend to use their judgment not to make sound decisions but as a tool against others. The main reason to get out of a judgment mindset is that it will generally bring along a scarcity mentality—one of never having or being "enough."

> *I have no special talents.*
> *I am only passionately curious.*
> —ALBERT EINSTEIN

Curiosity: A desire to learn, explore, and become enlightened, asking questions to gain information in order to arrive at a logical conclusion.

When you come from curiosity, you approach situations with a sense of wonder and a desire to understand the person or the world around you. Curiosity amplifies gratitude and enhances both creativity and problem-solving skills, leading to a greater sense of fulfillment.

Decision Point: Nonjudgment takes practice, so give yourself a break when it doesn't happen overnight. You are training your brain to think differently. It helps to realize that within each person you encounter lies an untold story. Here are steps to move toward curiosity:

- Refrain from making assumptions. Ask questions instead.

- Embrace uncertainty, not needing to have all the answers.

- Practice letting go of the need to be right.

- Seek out new experiences.

- Practice self-reflection.

FEAR VS. FAITH

Though faith and fear are beliefs imbued with emotion, and not a mindset per se, I am including them in this chapter due to the significant role they play in shaping who we are and the mindsets we hold. When you are rooted in faith, you have the power to infuse life with purpose, meaning, and fulfillment. Faith fosters a positive, abundant, confident, grateful, and humble mindset.

Thoughts and beliefs based in fear foster negative, scarcity, doubtful, and judgmental mindsets, which can even creep into entitlement.

> *Limits, like fear,*
> *are often an illusion.*
> —MICHAEL JORDAN

Fear: You are always concerned things will not go as planned, and therefore you want not only plan B but plans C, D, and maybe even F. Instead of focusing on the experience at hand, you worry about what could go wrong.

> *You don't have to see*
> *the whole staircase,*
> *just take the first step.*
> —MARTIN LUTHER KING JR.

Faith: You show loyalty and trustworthiness that doesn't sway. Whether it be in a job, a relationship, or in your spiritual principles, you allow faith to guide your decisions and actions. You believe things will work out the way they are supposed to.

Faith gives you strength; fear leaves you powerless.

Decision Point: It's exciting to watch someone move from fear to faith. Faith overflows into our mindsets—in fact, it flows into all areas of life. Take your next steps toward greater faith:

- Remember you cannot move past something if you do not acknowledge it exists. So identify the things that are causing your fear.

- Work to be in the present moment.

- Nurture positive self-talk to cultivate and strengthen your belief in positivity.

- Write your fear(s) down on paper and then burn the paper. Sometimes physically watching your fears melt away helps to eliminate them.

- Practice living in your fear for a moment. Look for ways to do the things that scare you on a small scale.

- Look for facts to help you fight fear and bolster your faith. We cannot be certain about all things, but oftentimes our fears are rooted in misunderstanding or a lack of information.

DARE YOU TO MOVE

Attempt to tackle all these mindset shifts simultaneously, and you might just feel like you're inside a pinball machine, bouncing all over the place and hitting land mines. That's why I recommend focusing on one mindset at a time—hopefully you'll move along more like a bowling ball toward a single continuous strike.

You might start by choosing the one limiting mindset that really hits home for you—the one that makes you shake your head and say, "Yep, that's me."

Trust the process as you work on change one day at a time, over and over, for as Earl Nightingale says, "Whatever we plant in our subconscious mind and nourish with repetition and emotion will one day become a reality."

Still curious about your mindset combination? Complete the assessment at becomingmorebook.com.

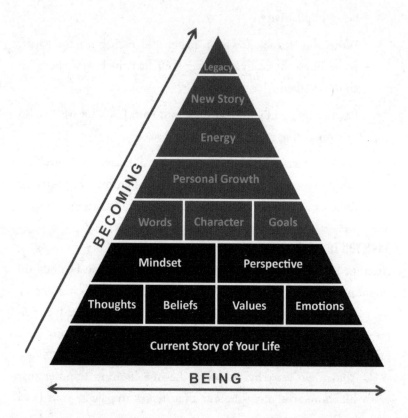

CHAPTER 13

PERSPECTIVE—
THE WAY YOU SEE

Everything we hear is an opinion, not a fact.
Everything we see is perspective, not the truth.
—Marcus Aurelius

Have you ever found that one parking spot so sweetly placed directly in front of the entrance and thought the parking angels were with you? Watching YouTube one evening with my granddaughter Marybella, we saw a great example of this. A gentleman was driving to the mall and upon arriving was delighted to see a person right in front of the entrance pulling out of a parking spot. He immediately turned on his blinker. No sooner had the car pulled out than another car seemed to come out of nowhere and zip right in front of him, taking the parking spot he had his eye on.

Imagine the emotions that he felt, imagine the story he was telling himself about what kind of person this guy was. He began to curse and was ready to confront the man and give him a piece of his mind. As he opened his car door and started toward the man to act on his feelings, the man turned quickly and, surmising the other's emotional state, said, "I'm sorry. My wife just went into labor and called me to take her to the hospital. Please forgive me." With that, he vanished through the entrance.

How do you imagine our victim felt now? In his mind, the last few minutes went from a story about a jerk to a story about empathy. As his perspective changed, so did his experience—and ultimately his story.

This illustrates an important truth: *all* experience is *interpreted* experience. The man waiting for the parking spot looked at the intruder through a lens that someone had taken "his" parking spot. That perspective was *his* reality. However, he wasn't alone. Even the man in the story who took the parking spot and emphatically declared that he needed to get into the mall to get his wife who was in labor was simply describing *his* experience, which was *also* an interpretation.

While you truly desire to believe that you can be "entirely objective" about anything, the reality is it simply isn't possible. The famous philosopher Immanuel Kant delivered us from this myth many years ago. Everything we know and receive through our senses, everything we reflect on within our minds, is interpreted experience. Every bit of information that comes to you does so through your filters, your grid—which affects and shapes your perspective in particular ways. Like that gentleman, you, too, can change your perspective and add one more step toward a new story and your legacy.

With each morning you open your eyes, look at a new day through the lenses of your perspective. As you already know, each block of the Becoming More Model influences the next, enabling us to build our life as large as we desire it to be. Some think that mindset and perspective should be the same block, yet they are not the same. While it's impossible to have one without the other, your mindset is how you think about, evaluate, and make sense of the world around you. Perspective is how you see the world according to your mindset.

Think about a pair of glasses. The frames are your mindset, the lenses, your perspective. The selection of frames varies as much as the lenses placed within them. Each lens allows the viewer to see the world differently—prescription lenses, progressive, bifocal, blue-light-blocking lenses, or sunglasses. You are constantly seeing the world through your lenses, which are continually shifting as you choose which lens you place in the frame of your life. Whatever lens you choose is how you will view circumstances.

A person who feels deprived and sees another person who has more than they have may believe the person should share their wealth with them freely. Their mindset is one of entitlement—they deserve a part of what someone else has acquired. Their perspective, on the other hand, is they may view the person as stingy because they will not share. You adopt a perspective that shapes everything you experience, and unless something puts a crack in your reality and allows a new perspective to peek through, nothing changes.

YOUR PERSPECTIVE IS YOUR REALITY

To demonstrate the extent to which our perspective shapes our reality, let's look at this Kanizsa's triangle (see the following).

Kanizsa's Triangle

Do you see a white triangle or three Vs in random areas? Do you see circles like pies that have a piece cut out of them or Pac-Man characters on the outer areas? It depends on your perspective.

The white triangle doesn't exist. Your brain allows you to see it due to familiarity of what a triangle looks like.

No, your eyes are not playing tricks on you. As you look at it, your brain is instantaneously scanning your past experiences and filling in the gaps that it believes are needed to make sense of what you are observing.

What you think you see is based on your perception of how you view the world and all that you have been exposed to. Your brain is bombarded by constant stimuli—sights, sounds, smells, to-do lists, people interrupting you . . . the list goes on. You prioritize tasks based on your perspective of what is most important. Importance could be linked to consequences, joy, love, empathy, guilt, worry, and so forth.

Your brain is a box of stories, written from your perspective about what has happened, what is happening, and what will happen. Is it possible, or even desirable, to change such a powerful thing as your perspective?

Yes, and yes.

Reality can be distorted by the brain misperceiving information from your senses, since perspective is influenced by cognitive and emotional states. This is why it is crucial for a leader, whether in personal, household, or organizational settings, to uncover reality. However, one cannot accurately define reality if they are solely relying on their own perspective. Contrary to popular opinion, effective leadership comes from curiosity and exploration, not judgment and absolute certitude. What does this imply? It means we seek to understand the perspective of others.

PERSPECTIVES DETERMINE REALITY

I once saw a study that showed 72 percent of people will allow the perspective of others to impact their decision to buy from a company or not. It went on to say four out of five consumers will reverse their decision based on reviews they read online. Perspective matters. Our own as well as others'.

Susan Scott, in her book *Fierce Conversations*, reminds us that no plan survives its collision with reality.[1] Everyone on your team or in your family owns a piece of the truth based on their perspective. If you look through a stained-glass window, you get a unique perspective that alters the view of the surroundings compared to what the person standing outside might see. It's important to consider multiple viewpoints in order to gain a more comprehensive understanding of true reality.

MOTIVATION ALTERS OUR PERSPECTIVE

There was a boy who had no motivation to attend school due to being bullied. His father wanted to help him focus on something else. Knowing he loved looking at the stars, the dad bought him a telescope and told him if he went to school, he could use the telescope at night. One day, as his father pulled into the driveway, he saw his son in the front yard looking through the telescope, only he was looking with the big end close to his eye!

His father said, "Son, turn it around and it will make everything bigger like it was designed to do."

The boy said, "Dad, I need to look at the bully this way so it makes him smaller. That way I'm not afraid of him anymore and I can go to school."

Which end of the telescope are you looking through? Do you have the perspective that the problem is larger than you are, zapping your motivation to advance? Maybe you need to turn the telescope around and see it from a different perspective.

---

[1] Susan Scott, *Fierce Conversations: Achieving Success at Work & in Life, One Conversation at a Time* (New York: Berkley, 2004).

> *Change the way you*
> *look at things and the*
> *things you look at change.*
> —WAYNE DYER

Sometimes taking on a different perspective helps you make better choices. What you focus on expands, turning your motivation in that direction. So pay attention to the things you focus on and ask yourself, *Why am I so focused on this? How does it help me? Would my motivation be stronger if I changed my perspective?*

PERSPECTIVE CAN BE DECEIVING

When the occasion calls, superheroes don their capes and put on their uniforms, taking a stand for something. Their ordinary life, represented by their ordinary clothes, retreats to the background and their superhero identity rises to the surface. They give the perspective of being human one minute, fitting in with everyone else, and by changing something about themselves they give another perspective of magnificence.

You may be like a superhero striving to act ordinary when you were born to be extraordinary.

On the other hand, unlike the superheroes wanting to make themselves act human, you may be camouflaging your humanity, acting like a superhero. Have you ever told someone you feel good, masking an illness? Maybe you have felt depressed, yet you leave your house, force a smile on your face, and give others the idea that all is well. Maybe you are living beyond your means, working to uphold what you think is everyone else's perspective of how successful you are.

While we often give tremendous time and energy to managing

the way *other people* perceive us, the one area that we rarely, if ever, think about managing is the most important one of all—namely, *our perspective of ourselves.*

Like Superman, we all have our own nemesis, our Lex Luther, who stands in our way. And I think by now, you already know who I'm going to say is your greatest adversary.

That's right. It's *you.*

You are the inescapable storyteller in your head, reaffirming or suppressing your own self-perspective. Like kryptonite, this narrative makes you weak, robbing you of your powers. Are you unwittingly using negative narratives to bring yourself down, accepting a range of limiting perspectives?

There's hope! You can reframe your story from a new perspective.

EXPECTATIONS AFFECT PERSPECTIVE

When you're expecting a phone call and you're in the shower, you can sometimes be convinced the phone is ringing when it is not. When a mother has a newborn baby, her perspective is that nothing else really matters. When she is sleeping, she won't hear anything except the crying or whimpers of her baby. She is expecting the baby to cry. This is called signal detection theory, and it was actually discovered while working to improve the sensitivity and perspective of air traffic controllers.[2]

Research shows that your perspective is highly influenced by the expectations you have set for yourself, others, and events. Through recognizing your priorities and embracing the emotions associated with achieving them, you cultivate a perspective of boundless possibilities, thereby enhancing your capacity to accomplish them.

---

[2] John A. Swets, *Signal Detection and Recognition by Human Observers* (Newport Beach, CA: Peninsula, 1964).

BECOMING MORE

In 2011, a study published by Alia J. Crum and Ellen J. Langer shed light on the power of perspective and how our expectations can alter our physical and psychological responses to work and exercise. They tested their idea with eighty-four housekeepers working in seven hotels across the United States. Half of them were told that their work activities constituted exercise and included improved health and fitness. They were given a presentation that showed how exercise does not need to be a painful activity, it's really about moving muscles and burning calories (about two hundred calories per day), and what they were doing each day met the US Surgeon General's requirements for healthy physical activity.

The other half weren't given that information.

Neither of the two groups changed any of their behavior patterns, nor did their workloads change. None of them conducted any more or less exercise outside of work than before. Yet after only four weeks, those who knew their work was actually good exercise lost an average of two pounds! Not only that, but their blood pressure also lowered, and they were significantly healthier in body mass index (BMI). They all reported feeling more energized and less tired at the end of the day, as compared to the other group, who showed very little or no change. This revealed that beliefs and expectations can absolutely affect the body and mind. It all came down to perspective—how each group saw their job and what they expected to get out of work each day.[3]

> *We often don't see things as they are*
> *—we see them as we are.*
>
> —Anais Nin

---

[3] Alia J. Crum and Ellen J. Langer, "Mind-set Matters: Exercise and the Placebo Effect," *Psychological Science* 18, no. 2 (2007): 165–71, https://dash.harvard.edu/handle/1/3196007.

PERSPECTIVE OF OURSELVES

How well do you perceive your own ability? It is an interesting question, especially around a task at hand. The term *metacognition*, often described as "thinking about thinking" or the awareness of one's thought processes and beliefs, shows us the void we sometimes have in our perspective about our own abilities.

Dr. Stephen Chew, a cognitive psychologist and professor of psychology at Samford University in Birmingham, Alabama, conducted a study in which students took a test and then, without knowing the results, predicted their score based on their perception of how well they did. The students estimated what percentage of the questions they answered correctly from 0 to 100 percent.

Dr. Chew then created a graph showing everyone's score based on their actual performance and on what they had believed their final score was. Each point represents a student.

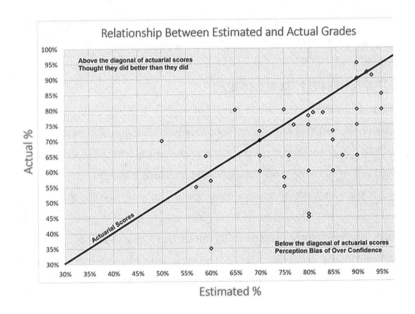

If their perspective was accurate, their estimates would match their actual performance. This showed up with the dots being close to the diagonal. If they did better than they thought they did on the exam, their dots landed above the diagonal. However, if their perspective was biased in overconfidence and they scored worse than they thought, their mark would fall below the diagonal. There were a few students who scored better than expected (at the top right and clustered close to the diagonal). Most students, however, did not do as well as they thought and had marks far below the diagonal. Interestingly, it was the weaker students who were the most overconfident. Their perspectives were not based in reality.

Remarkably, the students who scored the highest had the best perception of their results. The weakest students' perception was one of overconfidence, thinking they were better than they were. This is metacognition in action—perception of how well we believe our skills are compared to how much we still have to learn. Even having the perception that we are better than we are limits us.

PERSPECTIVE HELPS IN RESILIENCE

Your life's story will have times of joy and celebration, and like everyone, you will have seasons of sorrow and regret. No one escapes the fact that resilience is needed, and based on your perspective you will fall or become stronger during those dark times.

We can look at history to teach us how to handle these situations—if we allow it to. Doris Kearns Goodwin, a great political historian and author, often talks about our US presidents and how, despite many setbacks, their perception aided in their tremendous resilience. She writes,

More important than what happened to them was how they responded to these reversals, how they managed in various ways to put themselves back together, how these watershed experiences at first impeded, then deepened and finally and decisively molded their leadership.[4]

Abraham Lincoln suffered many defeats, yet his perspective was always to keep moving forward. On many occasions, he used humor to change others' perspectives. When he was ill with a form of smallpox, he quipped that so many people were asking him to give them something, and now he was happy he finally had something he could give! He added that though the illness could leave scars, he didn't have to worry because scars would not be able to disfigure him.

Observing a particular debate served as an exemplary demonstration of the ability to transform a negative perspective directed against you into a personal advantage. It happened in 1984, when President Ronald Reagan was running for reelection. Many were voicing the perspective of Reagan (who was seventy-three) as being too old to withstand the rigorous schedule needed as well as the competency to make important decisions that would affect our country. When his age became an issue against a younger Walter Mondale, Reagan found a way to use this perspective to his advantage. In the second debate the moderator referenced how President Kennedy went days on end with very little sleep during the Cuban missile crisis, ending the question with, "Are there any doubts in your mind that you would be able to function in such circumstances?" President Reagan replied, "I will not make age an issue of this campaign. I am not going to exploit, for political purposes, my opponent's youth and inexperience."

---

[4] Doris Kearns Goodwin, *Leadership in Turbulent Times: Lessons from the Presidents* (New York: Penguin, 2019).

Just like President Reagan, you, too, can flip the perspective from one that is limiting to one that is liberating, no matter what circumstances you are in.

Your position in life is based on your *perspective.* You may have heard the saying "Fake it 'til you make it." This implies that you might strive to create an impression that things are good even when they are not. Instead, follow this saying:

> *Face it 'til you make it.*
> —Dr. Henry Cloud

Face the facts and work through the challenge. After all, if your house is on fire you don't sit at the kitchen table having coffee and pretending you won't get burned. Like all the other blocks on the Becoming More Model, there are limiting and liberating perspectives. Become aware of your perspective and determine if it is serving you.

Limiting vs. Liberating Perspectives

Limiting Perspectives	Liberating Perspectives
Self-centered	Serving others
Narrow	Open
Problem-focused	Creating your desire
Low self-esteem	Confidence
Negative talk	Focusing on the positive

THE THREE CHAIRS

As we wrap up this chapter, let's take a look at the role perspective plays when we encounter disagreements with others. Resolution of conflicts and tensions usually requires the ability to get into the other person's world and see things from their point of view. We are often so deeply involved in our own world that we completely overlook the experiences of others. Here is a powerful tool that can aid in broadening your viewpoint entering the perspective of someone else's world. It can also facilitate conflict resolution within your family, workplace, and beyond.

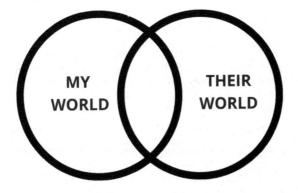

Worldview © Dianna Kokoszka

Figure 12: The worldview consists of your world and their world at the intersection of where the two meet.

Let me share with you how it works by relating an experience of conflict encountered by a team member of mine named Katie. The exercise we used to eradicate the issues started by setting three chairs in an upside-down U formation: one at the base of the letter and one on each side facing the other.

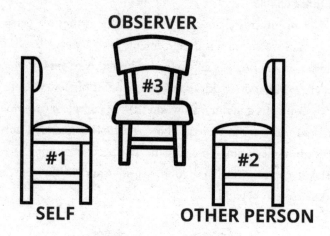

The Three Chair Model

Figure 13: The Three Chair Model facilitates the exploration of diverse perspectives in order to navigate conflicts and gain a deeper understanding of others' viewpoints.

I asked Katie to sit in the "self" chair (#1) and describe her experience and the issue from her perspective. After she was finished, I asked if she observed anything new or different regarding the situation. Subsequently, it was important to discover the specific positive outcome she desired.

After these questions were answered, I asked Katie a few unrelated questions to clear her mind and emotions and then had her move to the "other person" chair (#2).

"Now describe the events from the standpoint of the other person," I said. Following her depiction I asked, "Did you perceive anything new about the experience? What positive outcome do you believe they are striving for?"

Once again, having Katie answer some light questions to clear her mind, I finally asked her to transition to the "observer" chair (#3).

I then asked, "As the observer of these two perspectives, the 'self' and the 'other person,' which viewpoint do you think would be the most valuable for the person occupying the 'self' position to understand?"

Following that, Katie resumed her place in the "self"chair. "If this situation reoccurs, what perspective will you adopt for a more positive outcome?" I inquired. Since your perspective shapes your actions, "How will you plan to approach a similar situation in the future?"

Afterward, Katie expressed how beneficial this exercise was, and its impact proved true as dramatic changes took place in the way she and the team collectively realized they had not fully understood or appreciated the individual challenges each person faced in the workplace.

You, too, can go from a limiting to a liberating perspective when you are willing to open your mind to a new way of viewing things. Change your perspective and change your world.

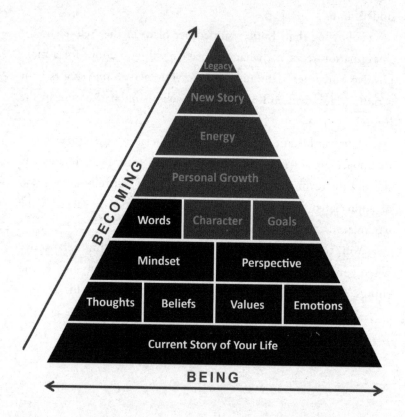

CHAPTER 14

WORDS—THE POWER YOU SPEAK

Words matter, and the right words matter most of all.
In the end, they are all that remain of us.
—JOHN BIRMINGHAM

Clint Pulver is an Emmy Award–winning motivational speaker, musician, and personal friend. When he was young, Clint was known as the "problem child" in school, always tapping his hands or fingers loudly in class. When his teachers advised him to sit on his hands to avoid disturbing the other students with his constant tapping, he would unknowingly begin to tap his feet. Clint became very familiar with the principal's office because he just couldn't sit quietly.

After a particularly rowdy day, Clint's fifth-grade teacher, Mr. Jensen, asked him to stay after school to talk. As the other kids "oohed" and "aahed," Clint knew he was in trouble, again. When the bell rang, his classmates grabbed their backpacks and left, leaving Clint and Mr. Jensen alone by his desk.

Mr. Jensen calmly sat down in front of Clint.

"Clint, do you think you can rub your stomach and pat your head at the same time?"

He could easily do it.

"Wonderful," said Mr. Jensen. "Now . . . can you switch your arms and do the opposite?"

With a curious look, Clint automatically changed hands to rub his head and pat his stomach. Mr. Jensen couldn't help but smile as he slowly said, "Clint, I don't think you're a problem. I think you're a drummer."

He then reached into his desk drawer, pulled out a pair of brand-new drumsticks, and offered them to Clint.

"But you must promise me one thing," he said. "No matter what you do, you will always work to keep these drumsticks in your hands."

As Clint held his very first pair of drumsticks, he said, "I promise," and his life was never the same. Today, Clint plays the drums all over the globe. He's a world-class performer and top keynote speaker. He has played for headlining artists and entertainers, been on *America's Got Talent*, and starred in movies with actors such as Jack Black and Jon Heder (from the movie *Napoleon Dynamite*).

One conversation changed his world, and one conversation can change yours. What is the conversation you need to be having right now? With whom? Who can pour into you? Who can you pour into?

And *what* will you pour into them? What *words* will you use? Clint had been called a "problem child," but it all changed when he was called a drummer. These words framed an identity—and it's one example of how powerful words actually are.

THE POWER OF WORDS

You really don't need a linguistics professor to tell you that words matter. After all, you hear them, speak them, write them, read them—yet do you think about them? Especially before you allow them to leave your mouth? What can you do without them?

I know what you can do *with* them. You can change the world when you use them to inspire, teach, paint a vision, lead to action, and encourage others. People grow into the conversations around them, demonstrated by Clint Pulver's transformation. Are you communicating with people in a way that inspires and elevates their growth?

Words of influence bring followers that can build unity or demolish futures. Martin Luther King Jr., who with one speech ignited the flame of hope within many, is an example of what the right words spoken at the right time can do. Over the years words have brought on wars as well as peace, built walls up and torn them down, taken men to the moon and returned them home again. Civilizations have been built and destroyed by the mighty word. Words are the context of how you see the world and are integral in building your story. Knowing this, do you consider the words you use?

STICKS AND STONES

Sticks and stones may break my bones, but words can never hurt me.

How many times did you hear those words growing up? I heard them more than once. It was often said with good intention to comfort me after someone called me a name or after a disagreement left me upset. The purpose behind the words was to encourage me to overcome it, move on, and build resilience, not allowing the harsh words to linger and continue to have an effect on me.

The reality was the words *did* have an effect on me. They hurt. Despite the positive intent behind the phrase, it simply didn't ring true. Moving on and forgiving was important, not for the people who spoke the words of hurt but for me. Forgiveness is an inside job not dependent on others.

Your words are pure energy, wrapped up and delivered in

bite-sized linguistic packages and hold immense power. They have the ability to heal or hurt, comfort or confront, educate or misinform. They are like a knife that, in the wrong hands, can do harm, yet in the hands of a skilled surgeon can be a powerful instrument to restore and heal, even save a person's life. The difference is found in the intent of the hand that wields it.

When communicating, the gossip talks bad about others. The person who continually talks about themselves, never allowing others to speak, is a bore. A brilliant communicator is one who asks questions and allows others to dominate the conversation.

YOUR BRAIN ON WORDS

In their book *Words Can Change Your Brain*, Dr. Andrew Newberg, a neuroscientist at Thomas Jefferson University, and Mark Robert Waldman, an expert in communications, wrote about the power of words on our thinking and our actions:

> By holding a positive and optimistic word in your mind, you stimulate frontal lobe activity. This area includes specific language centers that connect directly to the motor cortex responsible for moving you into action.[1]

Research by Newberg and Waldman suggests that focusing on positive words can alter the brain's functioning, particularly in the parietal lobe, which plays a crucial role in sensory perception and integration. They argue that the words we use have the power to shape our experiences and perceptions of the world and others, and can even affect gene expression related to stress. In short, a single

[1] Andrew Newberg and Mark Robert Waldman, *Words Can Change Your Brain: 12 Conversation Strategies to Build Trust, Resolve Conflict, and Increase Intimacy* (New York: Avery, 2013).

word has the ability to fundamentally change how we perceive reality. Therefore, when you are experiencing higher levels of stress than you'd like, consider examining the words you use both internally and externally, because the choice of words can greatly impact feelings and reactions.

HABITUAL LANGUAGE

Do you ever feel like your mouth has a mind of its own? Words seem to come out automatically? Maybe someone says to you, "Enjoy your vacation" and you automatically reply, "You too," even though they are not going on a vacation!

As you repeatedly use certain words, they turn into a habit and deeply embed themselves in your mind, almost as if they've taken root. The more you say these words, the stronger your belief in them becomes. It's like planting seeds, which eventually grow and bear fruit from which you reap the harvest. Your words convey your thoughts and create your destiny.

What words do you use over and over again? The average adult is believed to possess a vocabulary ranging from twenty to thirty thousand words. However, this number can vary greatly based on factors such as education level, reading habits, and cultural background.

It's not simply the quantity of words in your vocabulary that matters; the crucial question is, Do your habitual words benefit you? Are you inclined to use positive and kind words, or do negative ones dominate when they slip out unintentionally? Wouldn't it be wonderful if we could grab an eraser and eliminate certain words from our mental repertoire? Unfortunately, it requires intentionality to build a different habitual vocabulary.

To improve your life, evaluate which words you use to describe it. Which ones hold you back and which empower you? It's easy to speak without careful consideration, using unflattering and unkind words toward ourselves and others. Those words have a ripple effect, impacting the way we interact with those around us.

> *If you find yourself not being*
> *able to use kind words, at least*
> *have the decency to be vague.*
>
> —JERRY SEINFELD

WORDS HELP PREDICT OUR HEALTH

The word *conversation* derives from two Latin roots: *com*, meaning "together" or "with," and *versare*, meaning "to turn." Some conversations are so one-sided they are not "with" anyone; Susan Scott calls them "versations." When this happens, the words *I, me, my,* and *mine* overshadow what is being said. You tolerate it, yet your mind is longing to contribute.

A Harvard study revealed cardiac arrest is highly correlated with the amount of self-reference (I, me, my, mine) in a person's speech. The more we think of ourselves, the more we live with the risk of heart issues. How great it is to know that by focusing on asking questions, listening, and connecting, we can lower our risk of heart disease.

After reading the research on how words affect our health and how we care about people, I conducted a training to foster a more collaborative environment through conversations. The training emphasized the importance of asking questions rather than focusing on themselves and giving advice.

Each person brought ten one-dollar bills to the training. They were directed to circulate around the room and engage in conversation with one another, stipulating that every time they used the words *I*, *me*, *my*, or *mine*, they would have to relinquish one dollar to the person they were speaking with. Once they had run out of dollar bills, they were mandated to take a seat. I was astounded to see that within a few minutes, many of them had already sat down. Those who actively posed questions emerged as the victors. As a result of the training, many participants changed their focus from giving advice to asking more questions.

Can you tell me how many questions you typically ask during a conversation? When you speak, do you tend to discuss ideas and improvements and give compliments to others, or do you make the conversation primarily about yourself? The words you choose make a difference—even concerning your health.

WORDS CAN UNITE

President Franklin D. Roosevelt believed that clear and straightforward language was key to successful persuasion. Through his famous fireside chats broadcast on the radio, he knew every word mattered in reaching all citizens. One of his speechwriters used the phrase "a more inclusive society," which was changed to "a society where nobody is left out." Roosevelt also referred to his audience as "my friends," words chosen to create a more inclusive, personal, and comforting atmosphere. This approach helped him unite people together and ease their concerns and fears during wartime.

WORDS DIRECT OUR LIVES AND DETERMINE RESULTS

You know what can be truly beneficial during challenging moments? Embracing a helpful mantra such as "Things are always working out for me." Whenever faced with difficulty, expressing this affirmation out loud can contribute to creating a more positive outcome. I suggest you find your own personal mantra that will have a significant impact on how you approach things. No matter what you may be facing today, your words can determine your success or failure in any situation. Your words have the power to shape reality, not just describe it, so why not make them positive and uplifting?

When you change the words you use to describe yourself, you change the direction of your life, your career, and even your bank account. In his book *Facing Fear,* award-winning leadership speaker, coach, and *New York Times* bestselling author Don Yaeger wrote about Nik Wallenda, a member of the famous Flying Wallendas, a circus family that performed dangerous routines with no safety net. Nik was being paid $2,500 for ten to twelve shows, splitting that money with his team of multiple performers.

Nik was taking life-threatening risks every time he performed, but the pay wasn't matching up. Instead of complaining, he realized that words have power. Calling himself a "circus" act wasn't helping, so he started marketing himself as a highly skilled "extreme" athlete. That's when doors started opening for him. He was featured on prime-time TV shows, Discovery Channel documentaries, and more. His fame skyrocketed—and so did his earnings! Just a few words helped him rewrite his life story.

Advertisers know this all too well as they use words to spark emotions and evoke action. After all, which would you buy—a pound of hamburger described as 98 percent fat-free or as 2 percent fat? The words alone persuade you to make a choice as to which one you will buy!

WORDS REVEAL WHO WE ARE

The words we use reveal our mindset and perspective, evidenced through the different personalities in the narrative of our lives.

The Victim uses words that describe themselves as inadequate, not good enough, or about being mistreated.

The Villain uses words to hurt and manipulate others, gaslighting to gain power.

The Hero uses words of encouragement and positivity with "I am" statements.

The Coach empowers others with words of motivation and accountability, focusing on productivity and precision.

The Mentor uses words to educate, motivate, and instruct, weaving stories of lessons learned from their failures and successes.

It's crucial to realize how the Hero, Coach, and Mentor use words intentionally to move themselves and others forward, while Victims and Villains tear themselves and others down. Be deliberate about what words leave your mouth or keep them in your mind, invisible to others.

Robert W. Schrauf, an applied linguistics professor at Penn State, believes that our words indicate our thoughts and handling of emotions. He discovered that people tend to use more negative words to describe their experiences than positive or neutral ones. This aligns with the English language, which has a 50 percent negative, 30 percent positive, and 20 percent neutral ratio of emotional words. No wonder we use and think more negative words than positive. Some people are living in the story of "Goldilocks and the Three Bears," where complaining starts their day. Whether it's the weather that's too hot or too cold or they are working too hard or not enough, they always desire the "just right." However, the reality is that there is no such thing as a balanced "just right" life.

LIMITING AND LIBERATING WORDS

The words we attach to our experiences become our experiences affecting us. With research showing that words have a biochemical effect on the body, it only makes sense that the minute you use words such as "I'm devastated," you're going to produce a very different biochemical effect than if you say, "I'm a bit disappointed."

One lady I coached kept saying she was "depressed about . . ." I asked her to change her word *depressed* to "*working through . . .*" It changed her whole demeanor.

Another businessperson was always saying how frustrated he was. I had him change his vocabulary from frustrated to fascinated, allowing his brain to utilize creativity versus focusing on problems.

Want to optimize your health? The following is a list of word choices I've used to help others.

Limiting vs. Liberating Words

Limiting Words	Liberating Words
Depressed	Working through it
Need/Want	Desire
Afraid	Confident
Try	Working on
Have to/Should	Get to/Could
But–Can be both limiting/liberating*	And
Hope–Can be both limiting/liberating**	Trust
Frustrated	Fascinated
Should have	Next time
Can't	Can or will work at it
Can't wait to	Looking forward to

*Be mindful of your intent when using the word *but*, especially after a compliment, such as "Your dress is beautiful, but . . ." whatever you say after generally negates the positive compliment. Saying

"Your dress is beautiful, *and*" keeps a positive vibe going. When desiring to contrast what you said, then use *but*.

**Hope* and *trust* are powerful words that evoke different emotions. When used in the context of faith, hope is liberating. Yet when you say, "I *hope* you can do the job," it's a wishful statement. "I *trust* you can do the job" conveys confidence and belief. So, if you desire to emphasize the positive and give a confidence boost, use "I trust . . ."

Although the word *don't* isn't classified as limiting or liberating, it's worth mentioning that the brain doesn't register the word *don't*. If you're told, "Don't think of a dog"—really, *don't* think of a dog—did you think of one?

Every time you use the words *should have*—I *should have* done this, or I *should have* done that—in effect you are saying what you did was "wrong." I don't think anyone needs more wrongs in their life. Plus, using *should* over and over again gives you a "shouldy" life. We need freedom of choice and changing *should* to *could* gives us choice.

Want to improve your word choice and habitual vocabulary? Go on a liberating word diet! Every time you catch yourself using a negative, limiting word or catch yourself complaining, snap your fingers as you consciously modify what you just said. As you perform this act, it will be a reminder to switch your limiting words to liberating ones. Practice this and soon you'll find yourself naturally choosing more positive liberating words and phrases.

HOW COMMUNICATION WORKS

Since 1967, it has been widely taught that communication is 55 percent body language, 38 percent tonality, and 7 percent words. This practice I learned and taught to others. During my research,

I found that these ratios are from a famous study conducted by Albert Mehrabian and depend on context. Mehrabian's findings were focused on how people communicate around their emotions, which is when body language and tonality always override words. Mehrabian emphasized that words are still more powerful than people realize. Think about today's world of instant communication where only words prevail—through social media, messaging, email, and the like. People then add their own tonality, which many times is the cause for miscommunication.

Let's look at each word in the sentence: "I didn't say Jane stole that."

- Emphasizing *I* implies maybe someone else said it.

- Emphasizing *say* means I may have implied it.

- Emphasizing *Jane* implies it was possibly someone else.

- Emphasizing *stole* implies she may have borrowed it.

- Emphasizing *that* implies she stole something else.

This highlights the significance of words, which many times have more importance than we acknowledge. Plus, the absence of tonality and body language shows that the way we construct words matters.

What exactly is going on when we misunderstand each other? And how can we communicate more effectively? We can begin by realizing the process of choosing a word is not as simple as it seems. Here is what happens.

MISCOMMUNICATION MODEL

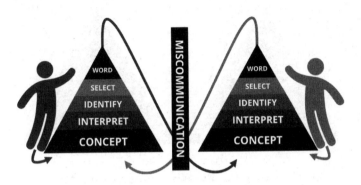

Miscommunication Model © Dianna Kokoszka

Figure 14: The Miscommunication Model illustrates the intricate process that occurs in our brains as we select a word and express it, and then the other person subsequently makes an interpretation upon hearing the word.

In your mind, you have a concept that you interpret and give meaning to. At that point your brain searches for potential definitions you have given that word, finally identifying and selecting the right word for the context being used.

However, the listener has their own interpretation. The cortex area of their brain springs into action the moment they begin to hear a word. They identify with it according to their understanding and related *experiences* around that word. They attach their own meaning to it. When you think about the complexity of communication, whether formal or informal, it's a wonder we can communicate accurately at all!

Even a simple conversation around the word *dog* doesn't give the same experience or meaning to everyone, as the following figure shows.

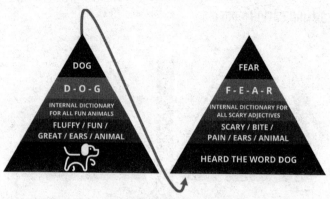

Demonstration of the Miscommunication Model
© Dianna Kokoszka

Let's say someone is looking at a picture of a dog. The person's brain accesses all the words and concepts related to the picture such as *animal, wagging tail, floppy ears, fluffy,* and *fun.* They then communicate the word *dog.* The person they are speaking with hears *dog* and instantly recalls a time they were bitten by one. The concepts they identify with are *animal, scary, bite, pain.* Their internal dictionary is different, so they choose the word *fear.* What was intended as a happy, fun conversation turned into fear. Two people, two meanings, leading to communication that goes awry.

THE RUDDER OF LIFE

With only a tiny rudder, you can turn a huge ship wherever you as the captain desire it to go—even though the winds are strong. Have you thought about you being the captain steering your own life by watching your tongue and the words it forms?

MOVE THE RUDDER BY CHANGING YOUR *I AM*

Many years ago, I had a meaningful conversation that lasted for hours with Don Miguel Ruiz, author of *The Four Agreements,* a remarkable man who emphasizes the importance of being impeccable with your words. One of my many takeaways was that people describe their experiences as well as themselves with labels called *words.* So I ask you: What labels are you placing on yourself? You will know the labels just by paying attention to your words after you say "I am."

I am are two of the most powerful words in the English language. The words that follow *I am* will always come looking for you. Think "I am successful" and success will find you. Think "I am depressed" and depression comes looking. The words you use shape your beliefs and become ingrained, like a tattoo permanently etched on your brain.

The good news is, you get to choose what follows the "I am."

Stating positive words after "I am" forms affirmations that label you as a confident person. "*I am* deserving of love and respect"; "I *am* confident in my ability and decisions."

Keep your words positive, for your words tell a thousand stories, give you purpose, and construct your character.

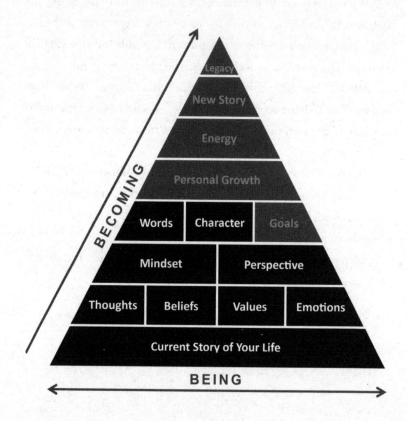

CHAPTER 15

CHARACTER— THE IMAGE YOU SHAPE

Talent sets the floor, character sets the ceiling.
—BILL BELICHICK

Your character plays the lead in a story called Your Life. And though you cannot have a story without a character, the character I'm drawing your attention to now is your image: the invisible mental and principled qualities distinctive to you.

Your character is not the role you play. It is how you play the role you are in.

In November 2022 at Exchange, a prestigious leadership conference, I and other attendees had the opportunity to work out with and learn from Navy SEALs. These men are considered *the* finest of soldiers—underscored by the fact that only 6 percent of applicants are accepted.

A hum of excited and anticipatory conversation filled the room as we thought about the kind of physical strength, intelligence, leadership skills, and character required to qualify as a SEAL—and as we wondered about what might be expected of us. How would you have felt knowing you were about to work out with Navy SEALs? Did I mention that it was raining, and we were headed outside? It was a little daunting to say the least!

As we were divided into teams, I took comfort in the fact that we were all in this together—come what may. Together we were challenging ourselves, opening our minds and bodies to learn new things and showing up ready to do our best. We probably wouldn't hold a candle to the SEALs, but we would bring our character out to play.

The bus ride started with a team huddle and a plan. Upon arriving at the beach, we stepped out in the rain ready to compete against the other teams. The first drill? A relay race. At the whistle, each team sends a member through the course: step through tires, use a rope to drag a large tire, carry a bag of weights, flip a log end-over-end-over-end, and finally, crawl under a two-foot-high net. Then, tap your teammate and send them running in the opposite direction from which you came. On and on it went like this, until each team completed the relay.

I watched as some team members completed the grueling course twice to fill in for teammates whose physical ailments prevented them from participating. And I watched as those on the sidelines shouted cheers and encouragement through the rain. It was a beautiful picture of perseverance and loyalty.

And the day went on like that, with each drill revealing strong character traits and many lessons about the values of hard work and commitment. From lifting logs over our heads to doing sit-ups and running up and down the beach, we learned that adding value, putting others ahead of ourselves, practicing resilience and decisiveness, staying organized, and paying careful attention to the details matter greatly in the life of a leader. And that's what we all were: leaders who were ready—now more than ever—to maximize our potential and work hard to positively impact our team.

Listening to the SEALs speak, it didn't take much to realize they possessed other desirable character traits as well: honesty, compassion, courage, and humility. And perhaps even more important: each man was highly accountable, took responsibility, and used reflection to learn and grow.

My favorite takeaway:

> *You've only got three choices in life:*
> *Give up, give in, or*
> *give it all you've got.*
> —Navy SEALs

Your character determines if you will give it all you've got to get results.

When we think about character, we think of how someone acts, yet people can fake character. That is why it is important to remember character begins internally and shows up externally.

CHARACTER IS A COLLECTION OF CHOICES

Your character is complex, developed by your habitual beliefs, values, emotions, mindsets, and perspectives. The words you use, the actions you take, and the decisions you make all influence your character. And when it comes to decisions reflecting your character, keep in mind that they may be big or small. They may be highly visible and affect many people or may be personal ones, made behind closed doors. Regardless, the result is the same. Are you aware of the ways in which your decisions define who you are to the outside world?

Everything on the inside shows up on the outside. On the inside, you are growing habits, integrating your character traits deeper and deeper with each choice, allowing them to show up on the outside through your performance and results. The more you make the right choices, the stronger that character trait becomes.

HOW STRONG IS YOUR CHARACTER?

If you were to liken your character to a tree, would it be strong like the wood of an Australian buloke tree—said to be the strongest wood in the world as it is resistant to rot and never weakens? Or would your character be more like a willow tree, tossed to and fro depending on which way the wind blows?

Every tree consists of a trunk, branches, limbs, and leaves all supported by a root system. Your character is like the life-giving roots of a tree. When the roots go deep, the tree stands strong through storms, evidenced by the mighty oak trees in New Orleans that withstood Hurricane Katrina and still stand today, giving shade and comfort from the hot sun. The depth of your character either enables you to withstand the turbulence of life or causes you to tumble to the ground, uprooted from all you once thought to be solid.

Roots, much like the foundation of a home, are developed underground, just as your character develops in private. With this in mind, remember that you don't need to brag about your character in order for people to trust that you are a man or woman of integrity. You don't brag about your character even though it is the foundation you build on, any more than you would call your friends and say, "I want to show you the foundation of the home we're building; the cement and rebar are to die for!"

No, you wait until the home has more substance: framing, a winding staircase, or a layout that showcases your love for entertaining. When your character has substance, it shines through on the outside—and people notice.

TRUE CHARACTER IS REVEALED IN A CRISIS

After becoming successful in real estate, I opened a property management division responsible for seventy-two houses. A friend joined me to manage the money by collecting rents, sending the mortgage payments, paying the sellers, and keeping a percentage as our fee. I thought things were going well until, one day, my accountant called. He had just returned from a three-month mission trip abroad.

"Dianna, we need to meet *now!*" he said, his voice firm.

"What's going on?" I replied.

"Do you realize you're out of money?"

"What?"

That caught me off guard. I took a moment to digest the news and then we looked over the accounting and worked to reconstruct the paper trail. What we discovered shocked me: my friend, who felt like a sister to me, had never deposited the rent checks from our tenants. She didn't use the money to pay the mortgage company or our bills. She sent out a few checks here and there to keep her secret safe and pocketed the rest. We had enough cash flow in the business for her to sustain this scheme for a few months before everything went haywire.

That same night, I left a board meeting to discover that my car had been repossessed. And boy, did word travel fast. A joke went around town that if you needed a ride, don't ask Dianna. You might not make it home!

So in desperation, I sold my business—all four offices—doing whatever I could to survive my costly mistake. I suppose I could have filed for bankruptcy, but I chose to take responsibility for taking my eyes off my money. It was important to me that I do right by the people who suffered due to my lack of awareness. I paid everyone back. I made sure every client received 100 percent of what they were owed. And I became a fierce negotiator with the bankers, making certain I paid back enough that no one's credit score was negatively affected. There were times I wondered if I would survive the sleepless nights and the many phone calls from angry homeowners, bankers, mortgage companies, and more. We didn't have the benefit of caller ID back then, so I had to take every call. After all, it could be someone looking to buy or sell a home. Because, yes, I returned to selling real estate in hopes of earning back the hundreds of thousands of dollars lost through my supposed-friend's embezzlement. By the grace of God—as well as friends, who loaned me their car to show property, and my children, who always acted as if nothing was wrong—I made it through.

That was such a challenging season. Yet through it I discovered the truth that character grows the most through trials, tribulations, and times of crisis. Peaks are about success and power—valleys are about growth. It is through both that your character is forged.

The way you handle your crises will determine the reputation you receive.

Want to hear the most interesting part? After a few years of working to pay off that debt, I made good friends among those bankers. If I ever needed a loan or line of credit, the bankers I had built relationships with were quick to give it. It surprised me a bit, until one banker said, "Don't you realize everybody knows you paid all that money back? Your actions spoke loud and clear."

Our actions always speak louder than the words we say. And this illustrates the relationship between character and reputation.

CHARACTER IS DIFFERENT THAN REPUTATION

Character is what you give to others, and reputation is what others give back to you. No matter how hard you work at it, you can never completely control your reputation. You can, however, influence it by your collection of choices and behaviors.

> *Character is like a tree.*
> *Reputation is like its shadow.*
> *The shadow is what we think of it.*
> *The tree is the real thing.*
> —ABRAHAM LINCOLN

Have you ever heard someone speak positively about a person, setting up an expectation of their character? If, upon meeting, their actions are consistent with your expectations, you continue to believe in their good character.

But what if you heard negative remarks about someone and then, after getting to know the person, found them to be kind and respectful? The reputation you were told about doesn't match the character you personally witness. Character is more than a report on a person's reputation, it's what you experience when around them.

Of course, nothing is so hard to gain and so easy to lose as a good reputation. A good reputation is fleeting in the absence of a strong character.

Character is about what you do when no one is looking. It's who you are *regardless* of circumstance.

CHARACTER HELPS EARN THE TRUST AND RESPECT OF OTHERS

People of character fulfill their commitments, take responsibility for their actions, develop others, and confront injustice. You can count on them. Authenticity, transparency, and consistency become their trademark. They favor giving over receiving, serving over being served, encouraging over disheartening. Can you think of anyone in your life whom this describes? May I suggest you spend as much time with them as you are able.

A person who is more interested in recognition and power than character is inconsistent, erratic, double-minded, and goes where the wind blows—so long as it leads them to higher places.

Lasting success is built on good character. This is an inescapable reality.

CHARACTER CAN BE CAUGHT AND TAUGHT

My parents understood the value of character and protecting the character of others. They taught us through their words and actions who they were and painted a picture of who we could become. One day, as I was working at the cash register of our family grocery store, a man walked in and Mom immediately said, "You won! You are the hundredth customer! Because of that you win fifty dollars' worth of groceries!" (Fifty dollars may not seem like a lot today, but in 1959, a loaf of bread cost just 20 cents and a sirloin steak just 89 cents per pound.) That night I asked my parents why no one told me about the contest ahead of time. Mom explained that the man and his family were having financial challenges and that was their way of helping without having him feel like it was a handout. Winning allowed him to keep his respect and dignity. In that moment, my mom and dad's character poured out from them and into me.

Like a tree planted next to a source of water, you absorb the character of those around you, the personalities you look up to, and the media you consume. They all become watering holes for you to drink thirstily, devouring your environment for sustenance needed to build your character.

CHARACTER IS SHAPED BY OTHERS

Look around at the people you spend time with, and you will find that your character traits are similar. Look at who your children's friends are, and you will see their future. The same is true in our own lives. Who influences you? What are your friends like? That is where you are headed.

And the opposite is equally true: watch who you are being, for those around you will become like you. What character traits are you pouring into your family? Whether you know it or not, you bear responsibility for the people closest to you.

Harvard conducted a study in which students watched a film about Mother Teresa tending to orphans, showing the characteristics of love and care. The number of protective antibodies in the students' saliva surged. When the students were asked to focus on times they'd been loved or loving to others, their antibody levels stayed elevated for an hour. Possessing the character trait of love actually makes us healthier.

Another study revealed that being generous with your attention can reduce your risk of heart attack. Wish to lower the pain you experience? Serve others. Lend a hand to people experiencing the same pain you have, and you'll lower your own pain. Scientists believe the release of endorphins explains the phenomenon.

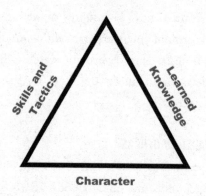

Figure 15: The Identity Triangle © Dianna Kokoszka

Describe for me a person you admire: a leader, friend, or family member (*not* their physical appearance). What words did you use? Take those words and place them next to the side of the identity triangle where they best fit. Words such as *Great baseball player* or *good dancer* would be placed next to Skill. *College graduate* or *smart* would go with Knowledge. Words such as *honest* and *brave* would fit with Character.

I bet when describing this person, you wrote more about their character than their skills and knowledge. And if they did the same exercise describing you, they would probably do the same. Character is often what people notice and respect most about us.

CHARACTER DETERMINES CAPACITY FOR SUCCESS

Talent and charisma may take you to the top quickly, yet it is character that keeps you there—or the lack of character that causes you to tumble. We can all become mesmerized by great communicators with charisma—and sometimes be disappointed when we discover their true character. This is called "empty suit" syndrome, or in Texas, where I live, "big hat, no cattle."

When appointing leaders, it's always best to choose character over charisma, no matter how impressive the charisma may be. People with great character will have true and long-lasting influence over others, what they do, and who they become.

LIMITING OR LIBERATING CHARACTER?

Research shows us that character traits such as curiosity, perseverance, gratitude, teamwork, and humility allow us to experience a more fulfilling, happier, and productive life. Scientists study these character traits under the umbrella of positive psychology—the study of what makes for a good life. It turns out that character matters big-time for both individual and societal well-being.

When you prepare your character, progress your character, and protect your character, you *prove* your character and produce outstanding results. It is important then to develop liberating character traits, those attributes that will move your story forward in a positive way.

Even a tree whose leaves are beautiful must shed those leaves as a strategy to survive cold weather or a dry season, knowing new leaves will grow when the seasons change. Likewise, you may need to shed some of your limiting characteristics to bring new beauty into your life.

Limiting vs. Liberating Character

Limiting Character	Liberating Character
Degrading	Encouraging
Fearful	Courageous
Indifference	Perseverance
Unappreciative	Grateful
Egotistical	Humble
Self-Centered	Compassionate
Any Unprincipled Characteristics	Any Virtuous Characteristics

YOU CAN DEVELOP YOUR CHARACTER

Anne Frank, a victim of Nazi persecution, wrote in her diary at the young age of thirteen, "The formation of a person's character lies in their own hands."

If strengthening your character is your responsibility, how do you do it?

In the same way you would follow a fitness program to build your body, you can follow the character fitness program and alter your brain to form a new character trait.

Your Character Fitness Program			
Choose	**Actions**	**Repeat**	**Obtain**
Learn/Have	**Do**	**Build Habits**	**Being**
Choose the character trait you desire to obtain. Learn its definition.	Implement what the definition says.	Be consistent in doing the tasks.	The new habits form a new you. You become the character you sought to emulate.
i.e., perseverance: steady persistence. Answer what it means to you to have that characteristic.	i.e., persist despite obstacles.	i.e., don't give up no matter what. This will transform the tasks into a habit.	i.e., you now persevere.
Portion of the brain used: neocortex (The learning part of the brain—I call it the HAVE portion, as it gathers and HAS the information.)	Portion of the brain used: limbic (This is the DOING part of the brain.)	Portion of the brain used: limbic (To build a habit it takes consistent repetition and dedication over time.)	Portion of the brain used: cerebellum (The BEING portion; this exists in your subconscious.)

Remember: Character is who you are *being*. It shows up in what you are *doing* and determines what you *have*.

Like every other part of your makeup that we've discussed in this book, character doesn't happen overnight.

> *Excellence is not an act,*
> *but a habit.*
> —ARISTOTLE

COMMITMENT HELPS DEVELOP CHARACTER

In summary, let's look at several specific commitments you can make that will be important (and effective) as you work to develop your character:

1. **Commit to add value to others, and value is added to you.** Helping others get what they want automatically helps you get what you want.

2. **Commit to forgive others.** This strengthens your character, freeing your mind and emotions from bitterness and allowing you to focus on what matters most.

3. **Commit to own up to your failures.** Taking ownership of one's actions, whether deliberate or unintentional, reflects a strong character and earns respect.

4. **Commit to go against the crowd.** There will be times when you will need to stand firm against the opinion of others or even what our culture deems to be acceptable.

5. **Commit to being intentional with your words and actions.** After all, your words and actions showcase your character.

BECOMING MORE

Setting goals is one of the first steps to plan how to BE, DO, HAVE, and GIVE what you desire. The second step is to *act*. Let's do both in the next chapter.

Character Traits I Would Like to Be Known For

_____

_____

_____

_____

_____

_____

_____

_____

_____

_____

_____

_____

_____

_____

_____

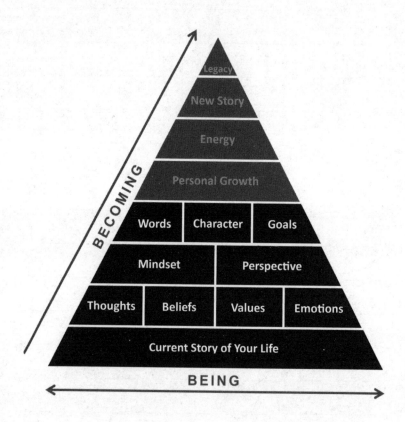

CHAPTER 16

GOALS— THE ENDS YOU PURSUE

"Would you tell me, please, which way
I ought to go from here?" said Alice.
"That depends a good deal on where
you want to get to," said the Cat.
"I don't much care where," said Alice.
"Then it doesn't matter which way you go," said the Cat.
—LEWIS CARROLL, *ALICE IN WONDERLAND*

A young man was taking the most enjoyable hike through a beautiful forest, looking at flowers, watching a squirrel cross the path, pausing to admire the view. Sometimes he would stop and breathe in the crisp, clear air.

He broke through some brush and stepped into a clearing. Suddenly he thought, *This looks familiar.* And as it turned out, it was—he had already passed this same spot an hour before! As he stood there, an uneasy feeling came over him.

"I'm lost."

Eventually, he found his way home. Among the many lessons

he learned that day was, you can be lost and not know it—until you do. You can think you're going somewhere when you're actually just moving in circles. And if the circle is big enough, it feels like you're moving in a straight line. It seems like you're making progress. And yet you're not. It's still a circle.

This reality highlights important distinctions at the heart of the story. It points out the difference between motion and direction, between activity and productivity, between going nowhere by default and going somewhere, on purpose and with purpose.

ACHIEVEMENT

What does it mean to achieve something? Achievement implies there is a plan—something specific, measurable, and time-bound that you are working toward. A plan implies that there's a goal, an overall purpose that the plan is designed to fulfill. And purpose implies a passion, a deep emotional desire that drives us, encompassing who we are, what we believe, and all the things that matter most to us.

Without a passion, a plan, and goals, your schedule could be full of activities and your days stacked with events; you may believe you are progressing, going somewhere. And yet you aren't—you are just *going*.

Like the hiker, you will eventually discover that you are going in a circle. What is needed are *goals*.

SETTING GOALS VS. PROBLEM-SOLVING

Problems can be a catalyst for bringing goals about, but problem-solving is not the same as setting up goals. Did you ever think you solved a problem to find out it was the wrong one to solve? When faced with financial scarcity, you may think the solution is to make more money. However, the root of the problem could be mismanaged spending habits, resulting in the scenario of the more you make, the more you spend. If this is the case, you'll never solve the problem.

When you focus on solving a problem, you are working to make something go away. When you focus on creating, you are working to bring something into existence. This shift from elimination to creation opens new possibilities, taking you from financial scarcity to wealth creation. When you focus on wealth creation as a goal (rather than just a solution to make more money), you begin to consider the bigger picture—how to save and where to invest to create long-term wealth.

Problem-solving and goal-setting may seem similar, but goals are bigger. They are one continuous race, not hurdles along the way. Life is about setting up goal upon goal as you *become more* and run bigger races.

Do you find yourself focusing on problem-solving because, quite frankly, problems are coming at you constantly? All of your busyness—seemingly productive—can hinder you from setting goals and becoming more. Live a life of creation and conviction, not caution!

Passion is what drives us to take action. The amygdala in our brain generates our emotions and assesses the degree of the goal's importance to us. Meanwhile, the frontal lobe, which handles problem-solving, determines details. Both the amygdala and frontal lobe collaborate to maintain focus and drive behavior toward achieving the goals you set, while simultaneously causing you to ignore and avoid situations and behaviors that don't.

When you review your goals regularly, neuroplasticity causes changes in your brain structure, making you more efficient in reaching your desired outcome. Interestingly, your brain does not change when someone sets goals for you—it changes only when you have complete buy-in on the goals they have set for you or you have set them for yourself.

ARE SMART GOALS REALLY SMART?

You've probably heard of SMART goals (S=Specific, M=Measurable, A=Achievable, R=Relevant, and T=Timely), which is a great approach to goal setting. I like the thought of this easy-to-follow plan, with one caveat.*

(S) Your brain loves **specifics**. Your goals must therefore be unambiguous.

It's important to be specific and concrete when you break down your goals. One study looked at ways to increase recycling efforts in the work environment. The first group was told they should "*Try not* to put bottles into the trash," while the other was told, "*Put* all bottles and cans in the recycling bins." Note that the first group was given a negative behavior to avoid, while the latter was given a positive, concrete, and specific instruction. Which do you think did better? The latter.[1] Being specific makes a big difference in outcomes.

(M) If you can't **measure** it, you can't improve it. So your criteria must be clear, tracking what you measure consistently.

(A)* Achievable is where I start saying, "Whoa." If you can achieve them, where is the stretch?

A report from *Inc.* magazine on a study in the *Journal of Applied Psychology* suggests that ambitious goals stimulate the brain. The higher (and less modest) the goal, the more likely it is to be accomplished.[2] Another report from *The Psychological Bulletin* states that 90 percent of studies show more challenging goals lead to higher performance. Set ambitious or aspirational goals that challenge you and demand you think bigger.

---

[1] E. Rabinovich et al., "Nudging the Green: A Field Experiment on the Effect of Prompts on Consumers' Recycling and Energy-Saving Behaviors," *Journal of Environmental Psychology* vol. 45, 2021: 192–200.

[2] Geoffrey James, "What Goal-Setting Does to Your Brain and Why It's Spectacularly Effective," *Inc.*, October 23, 2019, https://www.inc.com/geoffrey-james/what-goal-setting-does-to-your-brain-why-its-spectacularly-effective.html.

Other research, studying the efficacy of a challenging goal, backs this up.[3] Subjects were divided into three groups. The first group was asked to cut their energy costs by 20 percent. The second group was asked the same, but they were given feedback on their success. A third group was asked to cut energy costs by only 2 percent. Which group cut the most? The group that received feedback! The group tasked with just 2 percent reduction did not achieve any reduction at all!

Make your dreams so big that if they aren't met with skepticism and some laughter, you're not thinking big enough.

(R) Relevant is important, for it aligns the goal with your purpose.

(T) Timely gives us a time frame to achieve the goal. Remember to set another goal prior to achieving the last one or else you risk losing momentum. Goals are part of your race, not the end.

Make your SMART goals SMARTER by adding:

(E) Emotions are what you feel after you achieve your goals.

(R) Rewards are what both you and others will reap upon achieving your goals. Write them down. How will you reward yourself, and who else will be rewarded by your achievements?

SETTING GOALS

In setting goals, Sir John Whitmore has given us a model to follow. It's called GROW.[4]

---

[3] Becker, L. J. (1978). "Joint Effect of Feedback and Goal Setting on Performance: A Field Study of Residential Energy Conservation," *Journal of Applied Psychology,* 63(4), 428–433.

[4] Sir John Whitmore, cited in "GROW: The Practical Coaching Model Driven by a Powerful Coaching Philosophy," Performance Consultants, https://www.performanceconsultants.com/grow-model.

G = Goal: What is it you desire to create?

R = Reality: Where are you right now? This shows you the gap/chasm that must be crossed. Many people get caught in the gap trap because they don't go to the next step.

O = Options: What ideas can you come up with to achieve your goal? Another word I'd like to add for "O" is Obstacles. By making yourself aware of potential road-blocks, your brain unconsciously figures out how to get through them before they actually occur.

W = Will do: What actions will you take?

Research shows that taking intentional action (no matter how small) toward a goal in the first twenty-four hours greatly increases the chances of success.

CHUNK DOWN YOUR GOALS

In January 2008, Alex Harris and Sibusiso Vilane walked unsupported to the South Pole (about 702 miles) in sixty-five days. Harris, a South African mountaineer, was no stranger to such expeditions, having climbed all "Seven Summits" (the highest mountains on each continent). Later, Harris and his friend Marco Broccardo would go on to make history by being the first to walk unsupported across the Empty Quarter (Rub' al Khali) desert.

Antarctica was nothing but cold and blizzards with haze for sixty-five days—what Harris calls his most challenging expedition ever. After hearing Harris as a keynote speaker, I was intrigued. Curious to know more, my husband and I invited him to our home, where we asked numerous questions about what was crucial in remaining focused while walking 702 miles dragging a sled in icy snow and harsh cold.

"It seemed impossible from the start," he said, "but when we broke it down to degrees of latitude and then days and even hours, it suddenly seemed doable."

Their goal was set. They knew how long it should take and how far it was. They knew the conditions were going to be merciless. They set daily milestones to get there. Every day, they marked and measured their progress on the inside of their tent so they could see it every night before sleep and every morning before setting out. If they hadn't made their milestone, they would need to make it up the next day. In the end, he says, they only got to the Pole by keeping firmly in mind that one step at a time was what was needed. Day after day, drinking only olive oil for energy, the moment came when they finally reached their goal, illustrating how valuable it was for them to chunk down their goals into doable milestones.

VISUALIZE YOUR GOALS

Visualize in your mind a clear image of what your goal will look like when achieved.

My son Shon always loved American football. From tiny mite league to high school, he participated on multiple teams and explored various positions, including quarterback and running back. To him, one of the most challenging positions was punt returner.

For those unfamiliar with the game, a punt returner stands downfield away from his teammates near the line of scrimmage. When the ball is punted and spirals high, the punt returners position themselves to anticipate where it will land, often getting sun (or stadium lights) in their eyes, not to mention wind, rain, or snow. Once they touch the football, if they drop it, the opposing team can recover it. This is why a punt returner must have good hands, quick reflexes, and fast feet.

My son often described feeling isolated and a bit nervous in that position because it's difficult judging how close the defense is while keeping eyes on a ball high above. His ultimate goal was to catch the ball and advance down the field, giving his team an advantageous field position or scoring a touchdown.

He knew if he dropped the ball, everyone would be disappointed. However, if he successfully caught the ball and ran it back for a touchdown, he'd become an instant hero.

Imagine you are a punt returner with the ball soaring high above you. You position yourself to make the catch. What thoughts are running through your mind? Are you thinking, *Don't drop the ball?* Are you focused on the footsteps of the eleven opposing players closing in on you? How confident do you feel?

As a mother, I worked to remind my children that what you focus on expands, so focus on what you desire to happen. When their confidence waned and fear set in, I knew repetition was necessary.

This proved true at one football game. The score was tied. The opposing team called a timeout. It was third down and twelve yards to go. On the next play, they would likely punt the ball. The timeout only compounded the situation for Shon as it provided more time for negative thoughts to creep into his mind.

I immediately made my way from the bleachers to the field and approached a high chain-link fence. I shouted his name over and over again, but he did not turn around. I wasn't certain if he couldn't hear me or was just plain ignoring me. Finally, he realized my persistence was only going to intensify. Begrudgingly, he walked over toward the fence. "Shon," I said, as I reached through the opening of the chain-link fence, grabbing his facemask, "close your eyes."

"Not now, Mom."

Yet he did close his eyes. I said, "Shon, I want you to imagine right now experiencing the feeling where you catch the ball, you're dodging one player after another, then another and another, you break free to the sideline, you're running as hard as you can. Your teammates are blocking for you. You run into the end zone and score. Your teammates give you high fives, patting you on the helmet saying, 'Good job, Shon.' Open your eyes. Now go out there and score a touchdown."

And that is exactly what he did. After the game, he told me, "Mom, thanks. When the ball was punted, positioning myself to catch, I had only one thought on my mind: *TOUCHDOWN!* The fear of dropping the ball or the other team coming after me didn't cross my mind."

This experience reinforced for me how visualizing goals is significant in achieving them. He didn't score touchdowns every time, yet Shon would quote Ogden Nash: "'All's well that ends well' is backward. It should be 'all's well that begins well.'"

Making a visualization to remind yourself daily helps you focus on what you're working toward.

Life is like a camera,
focus on what's important
and you will capture it perfectly.
—Ziad K. Abdelnour

To advance in my real estate career and be known as a top-performing agent who helps families, I utilized visualization techniques. Reading the company newspaper's section listing the top agents, I typed my name and pasted it above the number one position. Taping my newly formed list on my bathroom mirror was a daily reminder of my goal.

Taking over the number one position didn't come easily. Disciplined and focused work was required. Scheduling priorities of specific and defined tasks and then following that schedule proved that *success* is scheduled into existence. What does your schedule show?

Do you schedule your priorities?

Do you have thinking time in your schedule every day?

Do you incorporate skill development?

Do you take time to reflect?

Do you study the success of others?

The secret of your future is hidden in your daily routine.

—MIKE MURDOCK

PUT EMOTION INTO YOUR GOALS

There is a powerful exercise when I first started building a team I incorporated. It was to help people accomplish their goals. They would write a handwritten letter to themselves and date it one year from the year they wrote it, as if what they wrote already happened. (Writing it by hand embeds it deeper in the brain.)

The letter begins, "This last year has been amazing because I was able to . . ." They envision all that they desire to transpire and they write with as much emotion, details, and passion as possible in the description: what they accomplished, what it felt like to accomplish all they had, who they'd become, what happened within their family.

They then addressed the envelope to themselves, placed the letter within, and sealed it. The letter was then collected and saved. One year later, it was mailed to them.

What is remarkable is how a considerable number of participants had forgotten about the letter and upon opening it were astonished how much of what was in the letter they had actually accomplished.

Once, a participant wrote about witnessing her daughter coming down a curved staircase beautifully dressed for her high school prom. When she wrote the letter they didn't live in a house with a curved staircase. A year later, when she received the letter she had written to herself, she was amazed at how closely the actual scene of her daughter on prom night resembled what she had envisioned. Yes, that year they had purchased a house with a curved staircase.

As she shared this with me, she seemed surprised, yet I have seen this happen many times before. This highlights the power of the mind and how writing down goals consciously lodges them in the unconscious, driving progress even when we're not aware of them. The conscious mind is the goal *setter* and the unconscious mind the goal *getter*.

GOALS HAVE TOLLS

The road to success is not easy,
but it is well worth the toll.
Work hard, stay focused,
and never give up.
—KOBE BRYANT

One evening in his small New York apartment, Jeff Davis watched a documentary highlighting the journey of Miguel Sanó, a professional baseball player from the Dominican Republic. Jeff loves baseball and was a great player in high school and college, yet playing professionally was not in the cards for him.

He was fortunate in his last year of law school to land an internship with the Commissioner's Office at Major League Baseball (MLB). Little did he know this internship and that documentary would change the trajectory of his life.

He no longer wanted to practice law. He wanted to go to the Dominican Republic to see what all the baseball hype was about. As he was riddled with student debt, little savings, a wife who was expecting their first child, and no stable income, this was a big commitment.

During the next two years, he took many trips to the island and worked hard to learn the business of baseball and how to scout and evaluate players. He built relationships with scouts and front-office executives and made connections with trainers that led to partnerships with their academies. He learned that for Dominicans, baseball represents one of the country's most significant cultural institutions. Young boys are taught from an extremely young age that if they work hard, train, and prepare extensively, they have the potential to sign with an MLB organization upon turning sixteen. For many, the dream of one day becoming the next Pedro Martinez, Manny Ramirez, or David Ortiz represents the pinnacle of success.

Jeff embarked on a business venture with no financial capital. The one thing he had going for him was his ability to speak Spanish, thanks to serving a two-year Christian mission in Mexico in his teens. He persisted, traveling for weeks, bearing all the expenses, staying in unsafe living conditions, and spending all day in baseball fields looking for talent, with no guarantee of success.

These are the tolls we pay to achieve our goals. As Jeff's

story illustrates, we often don't pay tolls just for ourselves but also for others.

Luis Feliz, a fourteen-year-old Dominican, was among the first players Jeff scouted. As a child, Luis spent countless hours each day practicing, fielding ground balls, using a glove crafted from cardboard and twine. Uneven dirt and rocky playing fields taught Luiz how to handle difficult bounces with ease. He was a gifted athlete with an impeccable work ethic that made him a standout player.

However, soon after agreeing to represent Luis as his agent, Jeff faced another toll. Luis injured his rotator cuff. Jeff and his family made substantial sacrifices to bring Luis and his mother to the United States to undergo a costly medical procedure. They covered the cost of specialists, treatments, and rehabilitation and provided their home for several months during Luis's recovery.

"It's hard to think of those first few years without getting emotional," Jeff says. "They were incredibly trying times."

In 2018, Luis was able to realize his dream of signing a contract with an MLB organization—the Texas Rangers. Thanks to the tolls that both he and Jeff paid, Jeff was able to jump-start his career, Luis was able to lift his family out of poverty, and the toll gates were opened for success.

Through hard work, determination, staying focused, and never giving up, Jeff has signed more than forty players to professional contracts to date and has helped his clients receive more than $20 million in collective signing bonuses. Jeff's business success continues.

"Our passion and drive can carry us through dark times," says Jeff. "What got me through all this was my love for baseball, my unrelenting desire to provide stability for my family, and the support of people who believed in me."

Goals have tolls, and the end result is always worth it!

GOALS HAVE IMPACT

Have you thought of how your goals will impact others? Ask yourself these simple questions:

- What kind of impact do I want to have on my family?
- My friends?
- The world?
- Myself?

Write down your answers to these questions by hand. You may be tempted to type them, yet Gail Matthews, a psychology professor at Dominican University of California, found that people are 42 percent more likely to achieve their goals by writing them down and saying them out loud versus typing them and having them hide among the files in a computer.[5]

PUTTING YOUR GOALS TO THE TEST

Your performance must outsell your promises. Having goals will liberate you from a limited future of vague wishes. I have always believed that a GSD degree outstrips all the other degrees. What is a GSD? Simple! It stands for "Get Stuff Done"! And this is the degree we all must strive for to achieve success.

Now that you have set big, audacious goals, and you desire to get stuff done, it's time to turn the fantasy of your imagination into your actual biography, forming fiction into nonfiction.

As a practical next step, take the future vision of your goals

---

[5] Gail Matthews, cited in Sarah Gardner and Dave Albee, "Study Focuses on Strategies for Achieving Goals, Resolutions," *Dominican Scholar*, February 1, 2015, https://scholar.domini-can.edu/cgi/viewcontent.cgi?article=1265&context=news-releases.

through the "9 Cs" by answering the following questions:

Curiosity. What new skills do I need?

Contribution. Who will my goals help serve?

Confidence. How can I structure the milestones along the way to grow my confidence?

Consistency. What personal disciplines and habits are needed? Did I schedule them? What tasks are needed and are they in my schedule?

Collaboration. Who can I enlist that will support me in the pursuit of these goals?

Conflicting. Are my goals conflicting?

Commitment. Am I willing to do whatever it takes? Not just what is easy or convenient?

Challenge. Are my goals challenging me?

Competition. Am I competing against others? Or (better) against who *I* was yesterday?

How do you compete at your highest level? Through your own personal growth!

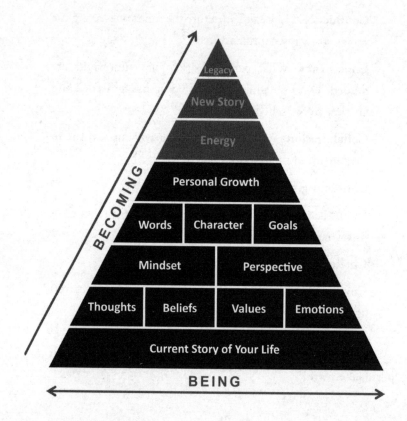

CHAPTER 17

PERSONAL GROWTH—YOUR UPWARD PATH

Growth is the only guarantee that
tomorrow will be better than today.
—JOHN C. MAXWELL

Goals are the markers we set to make progress in our lives, yet the goal itself is not life. It isn't about the goal you achieved; it is about the growth you received during the pursuit. After all, you don't go through life, you *grow* through life.

Life offers two paths: one of continuous growth, the other of stagnation. Which path will *you* choose? A coach, mentor, or a book can furnish you with some ideas, inspirations, and models for growth; only you can put your feet on the pathway and start your journey. Stagnant water stinks, so keep moving, developing, and growing.

Once there was a man who owned a remarkable racehorse. With extensive training and development, the horse grew to be the fastest around, winning every race. However, soon no one would enter their horses to race against him. In response, the man built a large barn to house the racehorse and painted a sign on the barn reading, "This is the fastest horse this world has ever seen."

As months passed, and with no one willing to race against the horse, the owner stopped training him. Finally, someone requested the horse to enter a race, but to their surprise, the once-fastest horse in the world came in dead last. The owner then took the horse home and changed the sign on the barn to read, "This is the fastest world this horse has ever seen."

When we prioritize personal growth, we stay abreast of the world around us. It becomes a place brimming with opportunities. Nonetheless, achieving success on this journey requires us to be mindful of who we seek advice and direction from.

For instance, my father sold tickets for American Motivational Association events featuring a variety of professional speakers. This gave me the privilege of meeting several renowned figures, including Zig Ziglar, Jim Rohn, Nido Qubein, Phyllis George, Art Linkletter, Dr. Norman Vincent Peale, and more. Many joined us for dinner at our home. Being in the company of these inspirational individuals was a transformative experience as it helped foster my personal growth and nourished my mind with positivity.

One evening Zig Ziglar was visiting our home and I vividly remember a story he told. He was in Birmingham, Alabama, on his way to Meridian, Mississippi. Due to detours and construction on the road complicating his journey, he found himself stopping at a gas station for directions. The station owner confidently drew him a map as he described specific landmarks along the way. As Zig returned to his car, the man assured him he should arrive within a half hour. Despite Zig following the directions precisely, one hour later he was still forty-five minutes away from his destination. He was there because a well-meaning individual gave him the wrong directions. Zig could have blamed the owner of the station for where he was, yet Zig knew it was his responsibility since he had chosen to listen to him and follow his direction. After all, you don't blame your way to a better life, you take responsibility and grow your way to a better life.

The moral of the story, Zig told me, was, "Dianna, be careful who you choose to listen to in the journey of your life."

This story taught me the importance of being deliberate in my personal growth by seeking advice from those who not only have answers—they have the *right* answers!

If you are not being who you desire to be, doing what you desire to do, having what you desire to have, and giving what you desire to give, then it could well be that your personal growth can use a shot in the arm with great thought leaders. Who are you listening to? Are you paying attention to the people who are guiding you? How can you differentiate between those who are leading you in the right direction and those wasting your time? Do their values align with yours? Do they have a clear understanding of your desired destination and are they willing to help you reach it? More importantly, do they know how to achieve it?

It can be difficult to determine if you are following the right people. Sometimes, individuals may sound confident, like the gas station owner, and may have achieved accomplishments that you aspire to. However, these achievements may not necessarily be in line with your values, beliefs, or goals. It's possible that individuals who drive fancy cars and live in impressive houses may be living outside of their means, while you, on the other hand, may prioritize having financial security for emergencies or future investments. Remember, things aren't always how they appear, so it is easy to be misled. Before you take their advice, or choose them as a mentor, you may desire to consider researching their values, beliefs, and financial position.

KNOW YOURSELF TO EFFECTIVELY GROW YOURSELF

To expand your personal growth, it's important to have a deep understanding of your own self. A valuable model that aids in self-awareness is the Johari Window Model, which is often used in psychology as a tool for personal and professional development. The model divides a person's self-awareness into four quadrants.

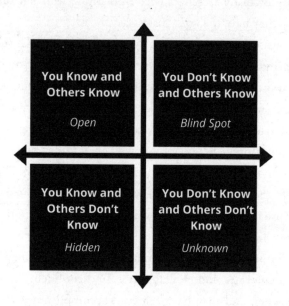

Figure 16: Johari Window Model

1. The "Open" segment is easy to comprehend. It encompasses behaviors, feelings, values, beliefs, anything you share openly.

2. The "Blind Spot" section includes aspects that are unknown to you. These items could be unacknowledged habits or perspectives that are observable to others, yet you yourself are not aware of them.

3. The "Hidden" portion includes elements of your character you know yet are unknown to others. Maybe it is your fears, insecurities, or even your accomplishments you are not openly sharing.

4. The "Unknown" pane represents aspects of yourself that are unknown to both you and others. These may include unconscious beliefs or emotions that have not been recognized. I tend to view it as the space where your possibilities and opportunities for growth exist—the potential that hints of greatness.

BE INTENTIONAL ABOUT GROWTH

Tom Bodett, an author, voice actor, and radio host known for his humorous writing and storytelling—including the familiar motel slogan "We'll leave the light on for ya"—reminds us, "Growing old is mandatory, growing up is optional, growing better is a choice." Although we cannot control the aging process, we can control our mindset and attitude toward life itself and the decisions we make around personal growth.

Growth doesn't simply happen on its own; you have to actively pursue growth opportunities. Are there limiting beliefs you have that need to be challenged? Maybe you have thought you'll naturally grow without putting in any effort, or you already have enough knowledge, or you must have everything figured out before you begin something new. Whatever is holding you back, overcoming these limiting beliefs is necessary in order to truly seize opportunities for growth.

Do you desire to advance your career? Maybe increase your bank account? Remaining stagnant or buying into your limiting beliefs will not suffice. Instead, grow where you are planted. Like a plant that outgrows its current container and has to be repotted to flourish, so will you move to a higher position with more influence.

Have you ever cared for a plant? It needs nourishment in the form of sunshine, water, and fertilizer to grow large enough to need transplanting. Similarly, you must seek nourishment in the form of knowledge and skill development to reach your potential, and yes, you, too, will feed on your share of fertilizer by encountering challenges and hardships that force you to grow. Trust me, your strength will be magnified during your most difficult times. Anyone can move easily through life during times of momentum; it takes growth to walk through adversity staring you in the face.

Be cautious about the sources from whom you receive nourishment. If the ideas and guidance they offer aren't good, wholesome, and beneficial, you risk stunting your growth. You may find yourself nurturing undesirable traits that obstruct your progress.

Find mentors who will challenge you on the unhealthy stories you are telling yourself: someone who will ask you questions that provoke your thinking, giving birth to new ideas—a person who truly cares about you enlarging your territory, helping you be more, do more, have more, and give more.

WHEN "NEVER AGAIN" MEANS YOU'VE GOT TO GROW

Every achiever experiences a defining moment, a time when they declare "never again." This drives them toward personal growth.

Michael Jordan didn't make his high school basketball team. This became a defining and pivotal moment in his growth as an athlete and as a person. He dedicated himself to personal growth in overall endurance and skills. "Whenever I was working out and got tired and figured I ought to stop, I'd close my eyes and see that list in the locker room without my name on it. That usually got me going again," Jordan confirmed via *Newsweek*. That one "never again" experience helped Jordan develop resilience and perseverance, driving him to success.

Over time Michael Jordan has become known as a GOAT (Greatest of All Time).[1]

Oprah Winfrey's experience as a news anchor in Baltimore, where she interviewed locals in different neighborhoods, was soon halted when she was demoted to the position of weekend features reporter, which she considered to be one of the lowest positions in the newsroom hierarchy. If that wasn't enough, station leadership asked her to change her name to Susan as they felt no one would remember the name Oprah. She refused to give up her identity and remained true to herself. Fate kept handing her blow after blow. Facing yet another setback, she was moved to a morning show called *People Are Talking*. Here was her "never again" moment, for she initially saw daytime TV as a failure. She delved deep within herself, harnessed her natural talents, developed her skills with hard work and resilience, and launched her own highly successful talk show. Today, she ranks among the world's wealthiest women.

May you discover your own "never again" moment, propelling you toward significant personal growth.

As Jordan and Winfrey can attest, "never again" declarations almost always follow failures. That reality underscores the importance of embracing the lessons that accompany setbacks. In fact, personal growth occurs less through our successes than through our failures. Bill Gates said, "Success is a lousy teacher." This reminds us to learn and adapt from our failures, *becoming more* than we were before.

Studying the lives of those who have made significant contributions to various fields reveals commonalities. They chose the path of

---

[1] Andrew Pistone, "Three Retired NBA Superstars Who Were Cut from Their High School Teams," GMTM, accessed March 2023, https://gmtm.com/articles/nba-players-who-were-cut-from-their-high-school-teams.

personal growth, which had a profound impact on their accomplishments, passions, and overall perception of themselves and others. Their learning, skill development, successes, setbacks, and losses all played a direct and proportional role.

A GREAT IDEA TO GROW

As a CEO, growth wasn't an option for me, it was a necessity, for I knew that a company's growth is directly tied to its leader's personal growth, and so the responsibility was mine. A lack of growth on my part would limit the potential of the employees as well as the company. Make no mistake, your business will grow only to the extent that you do.

When I first heard about a personal growth plan, I immediately connected with the concept, for learning was a passion of mine. I was already actively seeking personal growth by reading, attending classes, consuming various forms of media, being discerning of the people I allowed to influence me, and creating annual plans that strategically broke the year into months/weeks.

Years later, in one of my many conversations with Mark Cole, CEO overseeing all the John Maxwell companies, I inquired if he had been given any additional insights or tips regarding a personal growth plan. Mark graciously granted me permission to share the progression and the outline of the personal growth plan he uses today.

Mark Cole's initial plan consisted of three categories: books to read, experiences to have, and mentors to help him grow consistently (five total). He realized he had to be more intentional, so he added a word to focus on throughout the year.

After some reflection, he recognized the need to be even more purposeful. So he added the following questions:

- Who do I want to be now?
- Who do I want to become?
- Who do I want to spend time with?

Expanding his growth plan once again, he included five pillars, with each one comprising three distinct categories.

While the outline of this plan comes from Mark, the examples provided for each category are simply ideas I've given for your consideration and should not be regarded as prescriptive. Knowing Mark, by the time this book is published he has probably added more to his personal growth plan, for he is always striving to become more.

One of the best ways to ensure that your business grows and expands is to make certain that you are growing both personally and professionally. As Jim Rohn taught me, "Work harder on yourself than you do on your job." He is calling for a greater investment in yourself. What does this look like? Invest in yourself by making a growth plan and following it!

THERE IS ALWAYS ROOM FOR GROWTH

"Man in the Mirror" is a song I have encouraged many to listen to due to its compelling message.[2] I trust you will also listen, for you will see you have the power to effect change in your life and that you are where change begins and ends. Merely wishing life was easier is futile; wishing you were better is a step in the right direction. Whatever form your personal growth takes, this principle teaches us the bottom line—the best investment you can make is the investment in yourself. If any part of your life is stagnant, look in the mirror.

---

[2] "Man in the Mirror," written by Siedah Garrett and composed by Glen Ballard, recorded by Michael Jackson (1988).

Personal Growth Plan Example

Personal	Examples to Consider
Spiritual	Grow my faith (read the one-year Bible)
Health	Improve my health (hire a personal trainer)
Growth	Better myself (attend Maxwell Leadership Event Live2Lead)
Relationship	
Spouse	Weekly date night
Kids/Grandkids	Ask questions and listen, take trip with each of them
Extended Family	Monthly online call
Finance	
Spend	Create a budget
Save	Minimum 10 percent of income
Give	Minimum 10 percent of income
Calling/Career	
Business	Read business books, take classes, listen to podcasts
Ownership	Make an investment
Leadership	Attend a leadership conference, read leadership books
Community	
Neighbors	Neighborhood cookout
City	Volunteer for a civic affair
Church and Faith Groups	Give support/service/money

The more you learn, the more you realize there is more to learn, which allows you to stay humble, as you will never know it all. Therefore, learning is a continuous task you commit to for life. It is the one thing that will never go out of style.

> *Live as if you were to die tomorrow.*
> *Learn as if you were to live forever.*
> —MAHATMA GANDHI

During a workshop one day I asked everyone, "What needs to get better for you to have a better life? To have more money? To enjoy your work more?"

Unfortunately, no one said, "Me . . . I need to get better." But that is the answer. When *you* get better, everything else follows.

ARE YOU TEACHABLE?

A question to continually ask yourself is, Am I teachable? If you are, then let me again caution you: Don't learn from just anyone. While you can learn something from everyone you meet, be intentional about who you allow to influence you. Cultivate curiosity in yourself if you desire to embark on a lifelong adventure of continuous growth. Hire a coach or mentor to hold you accountable by developing some guidelines to follow, keeping them simple, demanding, and doable. Here are some examples:

- Do something new, outside of your comfort zone, weekly or daily.

- Observe your response to mistakes. Do you allow mistakes to impede your progress, or do you harness them for motivation to acquire more knowledge and enhance your abilities?

- Target growth in your strength zone, keeping in mind what you focus on expands.

- Always strive for growth; never settle for complacency.

- Hire coaches and mentors for guidance and accountability—those who will challenge you on the unhealthy stories you are telling yourself, someone who will ask you questions that provoke your thinking, giving birth to new ideas.

KNOW-IT-ALLS NEVER GROW AT ALL

The greatest obstacle to becoming better is not ignorance, it is the illusion of knowledge. Have you ever encountered someone who lacked the humility to admit that they don't know everything? We call them know-it-alls. We've all encountered someone who can pontificate about many subjects while remaining oblivious to their own ignorance.

This speaks to the Dunning-Kruger effect—a cognitive bias that causes individuals to believe they're more intelligent and capable than they truly are.

Researchers David Dunning and Justin Kruger, both social psychologists, found that a little knowledge can lead to overconfidence. Dunning suggested that the trouble with ignorance is that it can feel just like expertise. A tiny bit of knowledge on a subject can lead people to mistakenly believe that they know all there is to know about it. As the old saying goes, a little bit of knowledge can be a dangerous thing.

And while the unskilled overestimate their abilities, experts, on the other hand, tend to underestimate their intelligence. They believe they are not as smart as they actually are. Dunning and Kruger's research revealed that individuals with a high level of competence held more realistic views of their own knowledge and capabilities. Nonetheless, these experts tended to undervalue their abilities compared to others.

Dunning also observed that the very knowledge and skills essential to excel in a task are precisely the same traits that enable an individual to acknowledge their limitations in that task.

The Dunning–Kruger effect is not synonymous with low IQ. The reality is that this phenomenon affects everyone. Individuals who possess genuine expertise in one field may mistakenly assume that their intelligence and knowledge extend to other areas in which they lack familiarity.

Dunning and Kruger suggest that as experience is gained in a subject, confidence typically declines to more realistic levels because the more we learn about a topic, the more we realize we lack knowledge and ability. As we gain additional knowledge and become experts on that topic, we begin to regain our confidence. The question then becomes, How do we develop a more realistic assessment of our own capabilities, especially in an area where we may lack confidence in our own self-evaluation? Here are four steps we can take in that direction:

1. Continue learning.

2. Ask your coach or mentor for feedback.

3. Always question what you know.

4. Do research. Learn what others have learned.

It is also wise to consider the important differences between limiting your personal growth and liberating it.

Limiting vs. Liberating Personal Growth

Limiting Personal Growth	Liberating Personal Growth
Ego	Humility
Complacent	Curious
Know Enough	Learning-based
No Plan	Written Personal Growth Plan
No Accountability	Coach or Mentor for Accountability

For healthy, liberating growth to become an ongoing reality in our lives, it is essential that we move beyond ego and embrace humility. Ego is self-satisfying and stands for Edging God Out or Eliminating Growth Opportunity. For personal growth to be effective, allow your ego to serve you, not you serving your ego.

Another tangible way to nurture personal growth is by implementing the 5x5 program—committing to five activities for a minimum of five minutes per day.

Read: 5 pages or 5 minutes

Listen: to uplifting music for 5 minutes

Write: your top 5 priorities for the day (preferably the night before)

Meditate or pray: 5 minutes

Express gratitude: Reach out to 5 people per day via text, call, email, or note telling them why you are grateful they are in your life.

Of course, you can extend this to 10x10 or whatever number you desire.

DON'T LOSE THE GROWTH YOU'VE GAINED

Have you ever forgotten a password?

Have you forgotten the same password multiple times? Have you ever written it down and then couldn't remember where you wrote it down?

This is not an intellectual thing; it is an implementation thing. After all, if you don't implement and use that password over and over again, then why would you think for one moment that your brain would remember it?

If we're not applying the knowledge we gain regularly, we're going to lose it.

Don't lose what you have already been given by not expanding on it! Your growth will develop your new story. It will also contribute greatly to boosting the level of energy you will need to continue on the upward path—and that is the subject of our next stop up the pyramid of *becoming more*.

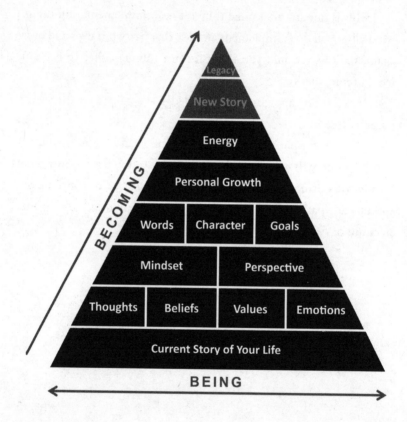

CHAPTER 18

ENERGY—FUEL FOR THE JOURNEY

The greatest waste of energy in our world is not electricity or fuel.
The greatest energy shortage today is the unused
potential within the lives of people.
—JOHN C. MAXWELL, FROM *THINK ON THESE THINGS*

Have you ever held a compass in your hand and wondered how this simple instrument, which has been such a useful tool for humanity for thousands of years, actually works?

I was in kindergarten when I was first handed one of these amazing contraptions. I remember walking around, staring in fascination as the needle changed direction. No matter which way I turned, working to outsmart it, the needle adjusted and managed to find true north. It was a thing of wonder. How did it know? What was this invisible force that caused the needle to move? Where did the force come from? If I went to the other side of the world, would it work the same way? I was intrigued by the fact that there are things in this world we cannot detect that have a tangible influence on the things we can see and experience.

My focus then turned to family, friends, work, and sports. It wasn't until years later that my curiosity piqued again. I was reading about Albert Einstein and how, in the first four years of his life, he never said a word, and he didn't learn to read until he was nine. Despite this, he ultimately became one of the world's most renowned scientists and made immense contributions to the areas of quantum mechanics, cosmology, and more—all because of a moment with a compass.

When Einstein was a child stuck in bed with sickness, his father gifted him a magnetic compass. Fascinated by it, Einstein would shake it so that the needle consistently pointed north. This inspired him to think about what could be behind the workings of the universe. He stated later in his *Autobiographical Notes* that this experience left an everlasting effect on him: "Something deeply hidden had to be behind things."

Though I wished I could have been as smart as Einstein, I was happy to settle for the fact we shared one common trait: curiosity. Quotes from Einstein and others were taped to my mirror. My favorite was, "There are only two ways to live your life. One is as though nothing is a miracle. The other is as though everything is a miracle."

It only made sense that when they offered a physics class at college, I signed up. Later, enthralled by this thing called *energy*, when they asked me to work in the physics lab, an ecstatic "Yes!" jumped from my mouth. I was so excited I forgot to ask if they'd even pay me!

Quantum physics opened my eyes to new possibilities. My studies finally enabled me to understand that the invisible force that fascinated me from my childhood had different names—magnetic energy, thermal energy, kinetic energy, and more. Regardless of the form energy takes, it is pervasive and dynamic, influencing everything around it. The awareness of energy patterns present in our world and the vast array of opportunities it generates are evidenced by everything being alive with energy, nothing existing without it. Not even you. Every one of us, from the smallest particles inside our cells to the cells themselves, is composed of energy, which I call God's energy.

Physics teaches that an atom is 99.99999 percent energy and .00001 percent physical substance, which means we are more nothing than something! It makes me wonder why people would fixate on the mere fraction of the physical world when our existence encompasses so much more.

You don't need to understand energy to know it exists. As you walk down the street in your neighborhood, countless energy waves—radio signals, TV signals, cell phone signals—surround you. You don't see them and yet when you receive a call on your cell phone, it is proof they are there. These signals may travel thousands of miles and turn a lifeless object into your personal communication device.

What is your choice of frequency you tune into as you drive around? Is it the sounds of SiriusXM radio? Or perhaps Spotify? You only hear the frequency you are attuned to. Have you ever stopped to consider the types of life frequencies you're tuned into?

Having learned that energy cannot be created or destroyed, only transferred or transformed, I began to ponder how it could exist within me, influencing not just myself but also those around me— my family, colleagues, or employees under my supervision. Knowing energy starts with self and radiates outward, I asked myself, *How is my energy being transferred to them? Can I control the energy I intend for them to receive from me?*

THE MATCH GAME

You may have heard that opposites attract. That might be true in some relationships, but not when it comes to energy. "Like" energy attracts "like" energy.

Have you ever played the Match Game? Holding a standard deck of cards, you place all the cards face down and choose two cards. If the cards match, you keep them and score two points. If you choose two cards that do not match, you turn them back over and remember them for next time that card is needed to make a match.

The object of the game can be applied to energy in our lives. If you desire wealth but believe you don't deserve it, no match! If you desire wealth and believe abundance and prosperity will come your way, match! You get to keep it. Positive energy will attract positive results—a match!

Playing the game with my granddaughter Marybella, I taught her that the energy you give out, you receive back. *For life is a mirror and gives back to us our own reflection.*

That is how you go about your entire day—playing the Match Game with your energy. No matter where you go or what you do, you are constantly sending and receiving energy. Signals that have a similar vibration are attracted to each other. Believe me, it is not chemistry, it is matching energy.

What energy are you sending out? Look around you and see what is in your life. That is the energy you are emanating.

In my studies I discovered that everything we do, whether it be the thoughts we have, the words we speak, or the tonality and body language we deliver those words with, can fit into three main categories of energy transfer: thoughts (cognitive energy); feelings (emotional energy); and words, tonality, and actions (physical or kinetic energy). The energy inherent in each of these can be transferred, unseen to the naked eye, and yet becomes concrete in experiential ways.

If you do not like what is showing on television, you pick up the remote and tap a button, sending an energetic signal changing the channel to what you like. You can even turn up the volume. It is the same with you, for if people like your energy, they will tune into your frequency as much as possible. If the energy you are sending is offensive to them, they will tune you out and find someone else to follow. You can turn up your volume, amplifying your energy through passion, excitement, and enthusiasm.

Have you ever found yourself talking with someone who is moody and then you find yourself becoming irritable? That's their energy influencing you. Some people are so negative they are energy vampires. They suck the energy right out of you, leaving you tired and drained, while at your expense they leave feeling better.

This is why I say 80 percent of your success is related to the environment you place yourself in.

Just as germs are passed from one person to another, so is energy. The question is, Is yours worth catching?

PHASE ENTANGLEMENT

Have you ever heard the expression "Birds of a feather flock together"? What this expression encapsulates, in a folksy way, is the timeless truth that *like attracts like*. People who put out a positive energy tend to find themselves surrounded by others who put out a similar energy. People who emanate a negative energy—always looking at the glass as half empty or never seeing the donut, only the hole— seem to find themselves accompanied by those who share a similar tendency for doom and gloom.

Like a magnet, you, too, have a stickiness about you that allows whatever energy you are sending out to attract the same kind to stick to you.

This is why you don't get what you want, you get who you are.

When two particles come together, they take a portion of the other with them when they part ways. This is called Phase Entanglement. If you're not intentional about maintaining your own energy when interacting with someone else, you will unintentionally absorb theirs. Science continues in many ways to put new angles on the adage "You become like the people you hang out with"!

MANAGING YOUR ENERGY

Have you ever been told to manage your energy?

Typically, when we discuss managing something in our lives, we hear the phrase "manage your time." This well-meaning phrase is said by people who are concerned about using their time efficiently. Since you have the same finite amount of time as everyone else—twenty-four hours per day—what if instead of managing time, you managed your energy, which is limitless, much like air?

Let's say you are home sick in bed. You still have the same amount of time, and efficiency won't help. The fact is, without energy you cannot accomplish your work. Physical, mental, emotional, and spiritual energy are required to make it through your day.

Have you ever experienced a moment where you were engrossed in a project and upon glancing at the clock, you were astounded by how quickly time had flown by? It felt as though you had only just begun. Conversely, when you are working on an unenjoyable project, time tends to drag on endlessly. It's not about time, it's about energy!

ADJUSTING YOUR ENERGY QUADRANT

To help bring this point home, think of your energy in terms of four quadrants: high positive, low positive, high negative, low negative.

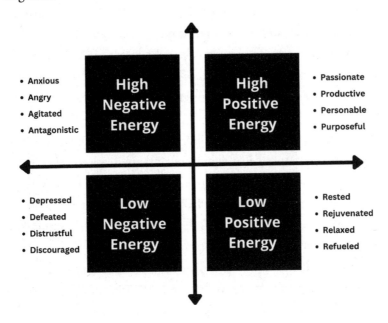

- Anxious
- Angry
- Agitated
- Antagonistic

High Negative Energy

High Positive Energy

- Passionate
- Productive
- Personable
- Purposeful

- Depressed
- Defeated
- Distrustful
- Discouraged

Low Negative Energy

Low Positive Energy

- Rested
- Rejuvenated
- Relaxed
- Refueled

Energy Quadrant Model © Dianna Kokoszka

Figure 17: The Energy Quadrant Model enables us to assess the current state of our energy levels, distinguishing between high or low positive energy and high or low negative energy.

You are always in a state of energy gravitating toward high or low, flowing from positive to negative. In which quadrant would you typically place yourself when observing your own behavior? Do you tend to have a positive or negative outlook, and do you typically experience high or low levels of energy?

It's important to recognize that it is unrealistic to sustain a

273

continuous state of high positivity such as perpetual excitement and joy. However, it is possible to shift between high and low positive states. Discovering efficient methods to restore and boost your energy levels can enable you to alternate between states of enthusiasm and serenity without succumbing to negativity. If you struggle to envision transitioning between positive highs and lows, consider the example of a professional speaker who keeps herself in a state of low positive energy until she steps on the stage, when she elevates her passion and excitement, transferring her high positive energy to the audience.

Suppose, however, you hold pessimistic thoughts that have taken root as a core belief about your capabilities. What emotions do you experience? Fear? Despair? Hopelessness? Naturally your energy levels will be dissonant, frenzied, or perhaps even depleted. As a result, you feel unnoticed, maybe even invisible, making your influence minimal.

Energy has the power to radiate influence both in your personal sphere and beyond. When you emanate positive energy, it spreads to all circles of influence in your life, impacting the success of your family as well as your workplace. Adding intentionality and expectations to your energy creates the ideal strategy to *becoming more*.

Have you ever considered the "energy card" you carry? Unlike your business card that you can hand out selectively, your "energy card" accompanies you, making a lasting impression on others.

NET FORWARD ENERGY RATIO

Imagine you're a pilot aiming to reach a certain destination. Just as an airplane needs sufficient thrust to overcome the drag of taking off as well as maintaining air speed during flight, your personal journey toward your goals requires a similar balance of energies.

The net forward energy ratio (NFER) refers to the productive energy (thrust) that propels you forward, fuels your confidence, and strengthens your belief in achieving your objectives. On the other hand, nonproductive energy (drag), such as distractions, lack of focus, self-doubt, or an excessive number of priorities, acts as a resistance to hold you back.

To determine your NFER, calculate the ratio between the positive productive energy divided by the negative nonproductive energy. It stands to reason that if 50 percent of your energy is spent doing productive activities and 50 percent is hindered by nonproductive tasks then your NFER would be 50 divided by 50 = 1—meaning you are standing still, no progress is being made.

Look at your schedule. How are you spending your time? Do you have activities that are productive? How many distractions are you allowing to get in your way? Figure the percentage of both. Even if you are 60 percent positive you are moving, yet very slowly.

This works for teams as well. You will need a minimum of 60 percent of your team with a "can-do" buy-in energy just to start to creep down the runway toward taking off (60 divided by 40 = #1.5 NFER). Get to 80 percent buy-in and you have a NFER of 4 (80 divided by 20). With this you have taken off and are flying toward your goal. When everyone is on board, well, that calculation is infinity, and the sky's the limit!

ENERGY IS A CHOICE

The energy you exude travels at the speed of light and is a product of your thoughts, emotions, words, and actions. Ultimately, like all things in life, it is a matter of choice. Applying these thoughts to this book's established framework, negative energy is limiting, while positive energy is liberating. Are you willing to deliberately choose to maintain a positive energy or shift from a negative to a positive one?

I challenge you to identify the activities that deplete your energy and stay clear of them, while also pinpointing those that boost your energy and prioritizing engagement with those.

Here are a few ways to elevate your energy. Choose one or more, practice them for one week, and observe how your energy is impacted:

- Stay in your gift and strength zone.

- Listen to uplifting music.

- Make time for religious or spiritual practices.

- Go on the liberating word diet described in chapter 14.

- Take part in hobbies or sports.

- Exercise regularly.

- Do breath work.

- Surround yourself with positive people.

- Make gratitude calls to five people per day telling them you are thankful for them being in your life.

If your energy is positive, then for heaven's sake don't change it!

In a perfect world, it would be wonderful if we could maintain positive energy forever; however, life is filled with trials and tribulations that are simply unavoidable. Have you ever found your energy plummeting? To bring your energy up to a positive level, it is crucial to intentionally take action and change the atmosphere.

Your beliefs and expectations help shape your reality, creating a self-fulfilling prophecy. For instance, if you frequently think and speak about not having enough money, constantly worrying, and complaining about it, your energy will align. Even if you consciously desire financial abundance, your subconscious mind may unknowingly set in motion a plan that perpetuates your current state of financial lack.

Our existence is characterized by limitless possibilities, and modifications in our energy can yield different results, as supported by the principles of chaos theory in physics, which focuses on underlying patterns in areas that were once thought to be random. The theory, for instance, explores how a seemingly insignificant event such as a butterfly flapping its wings in South Africa can trigger a hurricane in Florida. Tying this to our journey to becoming more, small changes in your thoughts can influence your beliefs, emotions, and words, all of which have the power to transform energy and ultimately lead to altered results.

Change can happen by changing the energy you broadcast.
Change the radio station—change the music.
Change your thoughts—change your emotions.
Change your words—change your direction.
Change your actions—change your results.
Change your energy—change your life!

ELEVATE YOUR ENERGY

Energy is one of the primary powers propelling you to become the hero of your own life. It's so fundamental to your achievements that there are numerous tangible forms of energy that can aid you every day. Each has the capacity to fill you with positive dynamism and ultimately steer you toward success. The following four types encompassed within God's energy can catapult you to unprecedented heights as you apply them to your life.

1. Energy of Intention and Purpose

Do you know if you're living your purpose? Some people believe pursuing their purpose leads to fulfillment, not achievement. When you are intentional about living your purpose, passionate energy shows up, allowing you to have the best of both worlds: achievement with fulfillment.

The distinction between being *off* purpose and *on* purpose is vital to recognize. Being off purpose is like playing Whac-A-Mole, where the moles continuously pop up and down as you attempt to hit one with a hammer before the next one appears. When you are on purpose, however, it is like continuously hitting a nail until it is firmly pounded and holds in place.

If you find yourself grinding it out day after day without a clear purpose, unaware of why you are doing it, the grind is likely to burn you out. You may encounter obstacles that knock you off course. Understanding the reasons behind your actions will provide you strength to persevere in the face of adversity.

2. Energy of Confidence

My friend Greg Smith once asked me, "What do you think is the most beautiful feature of a person?" At first, I thought of their smile or eyes. When he said, "Confidence," I realized he was correct. Self-confidence is a magnetic energy that sometimes can evade us. We can have great confidence around one thing and feel massive self-doubt in another.

Maybe that doubt comes from others placing labels of negative words, from unfair treatment, or from belittling that has diminished your confidence. It's essential to remember that others cannot dictate who you are or who you will become. God doesn't create junk or anything insignificant; therefore, as I've emphasized in previous chapters, you are a *masterpiece*, one of a kind. If you are going to be successful in creating the life of your dreams, you have to believe you have what it takes to pull it off.

You've already learned how to change your thoughts, so now you can work on positive thoughts about yourself and watch your energy of confidence rise high. It's about valuing yourself and seeing your own potential—and believe me, you are full of potential!

The energy of confidence arises from taking responsibility for your thoughts, emotions, and behaviors. However, this powerful energy dwindles when you start comparing yourself to others. Comparison is generally based on exterior factors, not knowing how others feel or what they are thinking internally. Authentic confidence enables you to uplift and encourage others through complimenting and speaking greatness into them.

3. Energy of Gratitude and Generosity

Research utilizing brain scans demonstrates that when a person is grateful, the regions of the brain associated with logic, creativity, and intuition, as well as joy and happiness, increase in activity. Gratitude also boosts serotonin and activates dopamine—which, as you probably remember, are both responsible for happy feelings.

Expressing gratitude for what we have, regardless of how little it may be, has a way of generating more things to be grateful for. Conversely, when we dwell on and complain about the things we don't have, we tend to notice more things we lack, and so we never have enough.

Many don't realize all the wonderful things to be grateful for in their life because their attention is focused on their troubles. This is illustrated by the well-known anecdote often referred to as the "black dot story." The author remains anonymous, yet it has resonated and struck a chord in the popular mind.

One day, a professor entered his classroom and announced a surprise test. The students waited anxiously for the exam to begin. Each person received a piece of paper face down on their desk. They were told, "Turn the paper over and let the test begin."

To everyone's surprise, there were no questions—just a black dot in the center of the paper. The professor, seeing the expression on everyone's faces, told them, "I want you to write about what you see."

The students, a little confused, got started on the task. At the end of the class, the professor took all the exams and started reading each one aloud in front of the students.

After all had been read, the classroom was silent. The professor explained, "I'm not going to grade you on this; I just wanted to give you something to think about. No one wrote about the white part of the paper. Everyone focused on the black dot—and the same thing happens in our lives. Some insist on focusing only on the health issues that bother them, the lack of money, the complicated relationship with a family member, the disappointment with a friend. All these dark spots are very small when compared to everything we have in our lives. Therefore, don't allow them to pollute your minds.

"Take your eyes away from the black dot," he continued. "Enjoy your blessings that encompass each moment life gives you. Gratitude brings joy and a life filled with love!"

Gratitude can also lead to generosity. You could say gratitude and generosity are a two-for-one energy package. In my experience everyone who practices gratitude feels passionate about giving to others, whether it is their time, knowledge, experience, or resources.

4. Energy of Being in the Present Moment

Do you know someone that seems to be "stuck in the past," constantly reliving old negative memories? What they may not realize is that by leaving the past behind, they can also leave behind the old energy that no longer serves them. Likewise, we may be trapped in the future, consumed by anxiety or worry. Both are giving away today's joy for yesterday's pain or tomorrow's uncertainty. The present is where the real power lies; dwelling in the past offers no solutions, while fixating on the future provides no certainty. After all, we have only twenty-four hours each day, and once the time is gone, we can never get it back. So use the past for reflection and the future for goal setting, but live in the present moment to empower yourself with great energy.

To underscore the point, remember that change can happen only in the present. You may speak about altering something, yet effective change comes only from taking action in the here and now. It's not a matter of saying, "I'll change tomorrow" and waking up the next morning transformed. Focus, intention, and action—in other words, being present—create a magical energy that yields significantly better results.

What is more, it's so important to be *truly* present. Have you ever found yourself desiring someone's undivided attention, sensing they were distracted, not fully present, not listening completely? Did they honestly believe they could do two things at once? Research has confirmed that multitasking is a mirage and divides the brain's attention, causing individuals to switch between tasks rather than performing them simultaneously. As a result, they missed important portions of what was said, so it is crucial for us to give our undivided attention to the person who requires it. Remember: where attention goes, energy flows.

MAKE A POSITIVE COMMITMENT

Are you ready to commit to growing in purpose, confidence, gratitude, generosity, and presence? Don't wait a moment longer, for the commitment you make today will start a chain reaction of favorable energy.

Filled with a sense of curiosity about how to help others attain optimal energy, I embarked on a personal research study. By questioning hundreds of individuals, I sought to determine which energies they believed were sabotaging their success as well as those that, if adopted and integrated into their lives, would help them overcome hurdles and attain new heights. Their top ten answers (not in order of most to least) yielded the following:

Limiting vs. Liberating Energy

Limiting Energy	Liberating Energy
Fearful	Joyful
Worried	Grateful
Nervous	Confident
Depressed	Passionate
Dissatisfaction	Approval
Anxious	Intentional
Stress	Responsibility
Complaining	Optimistic
Irritated	Resilient
Self-doubt	Creativity

When you honor yourself and others, you increase your energy. Every thought, feeling, and action becomes part of the energetic bank account you are constantly managing. Liberating energies are deposits, while limiting energies restrict you and are like a withdrawal. Which energies are more prevalent in your life—deposits or withdrawals? If you had an energetic bank account, would it be plentiful or overdrawn?

The right energy empowers the transformation from a dreamer to a doer, a pretender to a performer. You hold the capacity for liberating energy, which is essential for meaningful achievement. By nurturing and maintaining this energy, you can shape a fresh narrative and craft a new story for your life.

Remember, you attract who you are—not what you desire.

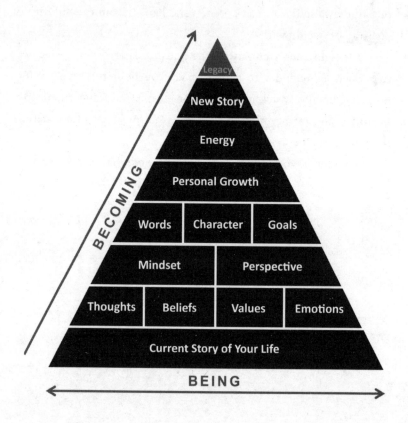

CHAPTER 19

YOUR NEW STORY— THE SCRIPT IS FLIPPED

This is my life . . . my story . . . my book.
I will no longer let anyone else write it;
nor will I apologize for the edits I make.
—STEVE MARABOLI

Holding a book in his hands, John Maxwell stared at its title, *The Greatest Story Ever Told*. It was a gift from his friend Eileen Beavers. With eager anticipation, not wanting to wait a moment before reading it, he opened the book . . . and was shocked! The pages were blank. Inside was a note from Eileen that read, "John, your life is before you. Fill these pages with kind acts, good thoughts, matters of your heart. Write a great story with your life."

That note served as a reminder to John that his life was still unwritten and that he had the power to fill the blank pages, creating a great story with the decisions he made, the actions he took, and the people he associated with.

This is what I desire for you. To live a magnificent story—one that surpasses all others. You may be thinking you don't have what it

10

takes to write the greatest story ever told, maybe even wondering if you make any difference at all. Well, think again. In fact, read below where the *e* key is broken on a keyboard.

> Whxn I think I don't makx a diffxrxncx in this world I think about my kxy board and rxalizxd that whxn the x kxy on my kxyboard doxsn't work it makxs a diffxrxncx and mattxrs trxmxndously, so just onx kxy makxs it hard to rxad. So whxn you think you do not makx a diffxrxnc think about the lxttxr on the kxyboard and know that you do mattxr and you do makx a diffxrxncx.

Although you still may be able to decipher it, the *e* does make a difference. No one wants to have a story of xxcxllxncx when they can have *excellence*. In this case, you are the (e) and you make a difference.

You do matter.
Your story matters.

REMEMBER THAT TIME IN YOUR LIFE WHEN . . .

You could fill in the rest of this phrase hundreds if not a thousand different ways. After all, your life is a collection of short stories—all bundled together with each of them penned by you. The question is, Now that you're on the *becoming more* journey, what are you going to finish the sentence with now?

Remember the story of Michelangelo in the beginning of this book? As you've been going through every step of *becoming more*, you have been chipping away all the excess marble of your limitations, discovering the hero and mentor inside—all the potential that has been hidden for so long. As you've been doing this, your new story has begun to emerge. You have continued to increase your net forward energy ratio, realizing that this process is not "one and done"; it requires consistent effort and energy.

Have you been telling your new story to others? Or are you still being quiet about it? Remember, you're the creator and crusader of your new story. Your story has transformed because of your unwavering commitment to the results you desired. Every personal change you embraced played a pivotal role in shaping your narrative, which has the potential to become the greatest story ever told.

And so, knowing all these things, the time has come for you to pull together the various aspects of *becoming more* that we have been exploring and see them flow as one, like the Rio Negro and Solimões Rivers, combining and mixing to form the mighty Amazon. Like that endless, ageless river, your new story is one that is bigger than yourself and leaves behind a legacy—and indeed a world that is much better because you have lived in it!

You may be pleasantly surprised at how far you have come. Congratulations!

OWN YOUR STORY

It may surprise you to learn that Sylvester Stallone is not only an action hero but also a respected scriptwriter. In the late 1970s, Stallone was struggling to make it as an actor. He had a few small roles here and there, yet nothing substantial. He was at one point even homeless, sleeping at the bus station for days with nothing to eat.

One day he watched a boxing match between Muhammad Ali and Chuck Wepner. Wepner was clearly the underdog against the mighty Ali. Yet he lasted the entire fifteen rounds, knocked out in the very last twenty seconds! Stallone was so inspired by the fight that he came up with an idea for a screenplay about a struggling boxer who gets a chance to fight for the heavyweight championship of the world.

Stallone poured his heart and soul into the script, which he titled *Rocky*. He believed in it so strongly that he refused to sell it unless he was given the opportunity to star in it himself. Studios were interested in the script, but they didn't think Stallone had the star power to carry the movie.

Stallone refused to back down. He was determined to make his dream a reality. He sold everything he had, including his beloved dog, for $50 just to make ends meet. (Reportedly, he bought the dog back for $3,000 much later!) He continued to shop his script around until finally, United Artists (UA) took a chance on him. The studio offered Stallone $125,000 for the script. He refused unless they allowed him to play the lead role of Rocky Balboa. UA was hesitant, yet eventually the company agreed to let him star in the film for a meager $35,000 salary.

Stallone went on to pour himself into the movie, which was shot on a shoestring budget of just over $1 million. The film, of course, was a massive success, grossing over $225 million worldwide and winning three Academy Awards, including Best Picture.

The story of Stallone's perseverance and determination in the face of overwhelming odds has become the characteristics of Hollywood legends. Today Stallone is regarded as one of the most iconic actors and screenwriters of his generation, and *Rocky* remains a beloved classic of American cinema. Stallone went on to write more *Rocky* movies and others, becoming the superstar he is today.

When you think about this one story, Stallone followed every portion of the Becoming More Model. Starting with his thoughts then progressed through his beliefs, values, emotions, mindset, perspective and on up the triangle with persistence and determination, changing Stallone's life. Through your new story, your life will change too. Believe in it. Persist in this belief. And when that story finishes, write another one! Keep throwing the punches!

Start today. Pick up the pen. Get out the typewriter. Load up the laptop. It's time to get writing! You are responsible for this, no one else. You are responsible to put in the training. You are responsible to get in the ring and keep going until the bell rings! While others will lend their assistance and expertise, achieving mastery is totally up to you.

> *When we deny the story, it defines us.*
> *When we own the story,*
> *we can write a brave new ending.*
> —Brené Brown

Remember, it's a process that takes time. This is something that Susan Scott taught me from a passage in Ernest Hemingway's book *The Sun Also Rises*. Two men are sitting at a bar, and one turns to the other and asks, "How did you go bankrupt?" After a long pause, the man finally answers, "Gradually, then suddenly." That is how your new story will unfold! At first you will continue in your life and feel as though you are making little, if any, progress. Then, all of a sudden, others will begin telling you how much you have changed.

WHAT HAVE YOU DISCOVERED ON THIS JOURNEY OF BECOMING MORE?

To help you see this, here is a set of self-reflection questions to regularly ask yourself and others so you can measure your progress.

- What are others in my life saying are the most significant changes they have observed in me? (Ask them!)

- Do people say I am more positive than before?

- Have people noticed a change in my words and vocabulary? Do I speak more encouraging and empowering words to others?

- How would I rate myself on controlling my "second" thoughts? (Remember, you can't control the first thought—you can control the second one!)

- Have I become more firm in my beliefs and values?

- Has my perspective changed to see the good in others?

- How has my character been transformed?

- Have I continued to cultivate my personal growth?

- Has my net forward energy ratio gone up?

- What are three things I can do every morning that will keep me on the path to writing a great story?

WHAT NOW?

Writing your story on your own will get you only so far, yet even Rocky needed a coach to get him into shape. In *Rocky III*, there's a memorable moment when Rocky has lost a fight and his confidence, and Mickey Goldmill, his friend and trainer, encourages him with simple words.

"Get back in there and hit him with everything you've got. You owe that to yourself. When it's over, I know you'll be the one standing. You know what you have to do. Do it."

You'll never win your fights without friends, mentors, and coaches. When a friend gives constructive criticism or correction, even if it may hurt or be uncomfortable, it is ultimately beneficial. To me this shows their loyalty to you and care for your well-being. "Faithful are the wounds of a friend" (Proverbs 27:6 KJV).

You also need more than a friend or supporter—for they will often sympathize and empathize with you. You need a coach or mentor. It needs to be a person who listens well and who will tell you things you need to hear *even and especially when you don't want to hear them.*

Perhaps go through each step of the Becoming More Model with a friend or mentor, reading this book together. Or go through it with your team. Take the mindset assessment online at becomingmorebook.com to get started. It's time to get your story written—without fear! And to find the help you need to get there!

All through my life, I've had the privilege of helping many people write their new story. It starts with making certain you know you are the creator, character, crusader, and champion of your story and that your life matters. People have told me that I've changed their life, yet it's *they* who made the decision to change their own life. We don't change lives any more than a gardener can force a plant to grow; we give people what they need, and if we're able, create the environment to support them to make the choice and change their lives.

Now that you've passed through the gate of "different," it's time to rip off any other labels that someone else placed on you. You choose your new labels. Maybe the labels of *gifted, determined, adventurous, resilient, resourceful, efficient, courageous, thoughtful, encouraging*—whatever words resonate with you.

FROM SUCCESS TO SIGNIFICANCE

As you progress in life, your focus will shift from striving for personal success to prioritizing the significance of impacting others and helping them reach their own purpose. You will enjoy seeing them savor the pleasure of their accomplishments as they take their own journey of progress and change. Craft your story of *becoming more* with lucidity, making it meaningful and unforgettable, imaginative and inspiring, purposeful and memorable, building into others. The next chapter will focus on this as you move to writing a legacy.

As you approach the end of the book, you'll get to decide if you feel you have accomplished everything you desire and have become all you can be, or if you might want to reread it (on your own or with others), working through the blocks of changing from limiting to liberating ways to live your life. This is up to you, but it should be a no-brainer, for *becoming more* is a continuous process.

Life is a continuum from being . . . to doing . . . to having . . . to giving. It never stops until that day it becomes your legacy.

I said it once before, and to me it is worth repeating:

> *You can't go back and*
> *change the beginning,*
> *but you can start where you are*
> *and change the ending.*
> —C. S. Lewis

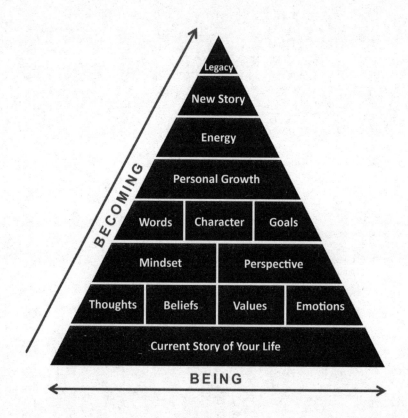

CHAPTER 20

LEGACY—
EVERY TOMB
TELLS A TALE

If you would not be forgotten as soon as you are dead,
either write something worth reading or
do something worth writing.
—Benjamin Franklin

During the Christmas season our son Shane, accompanied by his girlfriend, Jenny, visited Austin with the purpose of introducing her to us. One evening we decided to get out a 1,500-piece puzzle—forty beach umbrellas in five colors all placed in the sand. Needless to say, it was daunting to determine where the pieces went! Shane ended up taking it home with the portions we were able to fit together carefully packed. A month later he sent me a picture with the caption "FINISHED!" Sure, the top of the puzzle box showed us what it looked like, yet to actually *see* the puzzle it *had* to be put together.

This is how our life is. For each chapter of this book, you have worked on putting your life puzzle together piece by piece. Legacy is the full picture of your life that everyone focuses on when you are gone. Each piece is placed with what you do today, for they compose the picture people will remember—a picture that is unique, one of a kind, for you are a masterpiece in God's eyes.

WHAT IS A LEGACY?

When you google the word *legacy,* the top search answer appears as "Noun: an amount of money or property left to someone in a will or trust."

However, as we know, it's far more than that. A legacy is like planting seeds in a garden for future generations that you may never have the chance to witness bloom but will always be remembered for.

One year my mother asked me what I wanted for Christmas. It didn't take me long to respond with "your story." I longed to learn about the significant moments of her life. She graciously wrote down a portion of her life story, and I cherish it to this day. Upon her passing, my mother left only a few belongings to divide among us children and grandchildren, yet her fierce love and affection was worth so much more. One thing she created was handmade baby blankets with beautiful crochet work around the edges for each grandchild's children and their children, envisioning a future generation yet to be born. What does that say about the love she left as a legacy? This gesture proved to all of us that she yearned to provide her family with warmth and comfort long after she was gone.

When it came to our family, Dad's love was no different. He had a great sense of humor, was full of energy, worked tirelessly, and was very intentional about instilling values in us.

Their legacy lives on by what we learned from both of them: the importance of hard work and being mindful of our words in order to uplift others. You probably feel about your parents as I do about mine. I am truly fortunate to have been blessed with such a wonderful mom and dad. In an effort to preserve their legacy, I would like to share a poem with you that my parents frequently recited when I was young. It has served as a constant reminder to not lose sight of being a builder and encourager.

> *I watched them tearing a building down*
> *A gang of men in a busy town*
> *With ho-heave-ho and a lusty yell*
> *They swung a beam and a side wall fell*
> *I asked the foreman "Are these men skilled*
> *And the men you'd hire if you had to build?"*
> *He gave a laugh and said, "No indeed*
> *Just common labor is all I need*
> *I can easily wreck in a day or two what*
> *Builders have taken a year to do"*
> *And I thought to myself as I went away*
> *Which of these roles have I tried to play?*
> *Am I a builder who works with care, measuring*
> *life by the rule and square?*
> *Am I shaping my deed to a well-made plan,*
> *Patiently doing the best I can?*
> *Or am I a wrecker, who walks the town,*
> *Content with the labor of tearing down?*
> —EDGAR A. GUEST

CREATING A LIBERATING LEGACY

If you keep a poker in or close to a fire, the poker stays hot, but once you take it out, it cools down quickly. Likewise, it takes consistent and constant effort to form the habits and disciplines that create a positive, enduring legacy. Every brick of the Becoming More Model builds your legacy. You've been presented with limiting and liberating approaches for each step. Now, with all this in mind, what kind of legacy will you leave? Here is a simple, straightforward way you can answer that question.

A LIBERATING legacy is about

- Multiplying

- Increasing

- Growing

- Advancing

- Changing

- Adding value to others

A LIMITING legacy is about

- Shrinking/Depleting

Legacy is what you will leave behind for others. A good reputation cannot be manufactured; it comes about through your impact toward others through all these characteristics. A limiting legacy is one that creates shrinkage so that no one benefits. Remember, fathers and mothers give an inheritance to their sons and daughters, not the other way around. In each of the preceding liberating categories, look at all the aspects of your life, such as your

- Relationships

- Finance/business

- Spiritual and intellectual life

- Community/society impact

And then ask yourself:

- Have I multiplied what I have been given?
- Have I created an increase for the increase of others?
- Has there been growth of all I am involved in?
- Have there been advances in all my endeavors?
- Has there been real, measurable change?
- Have I added value to others daily?

A liberating legacy not only creates addition but goes one step further to *multiplication*. It's not sufficient to merely *add* to your talents and skills. Rather, you *multiply* them and pass them on to others so they can achieve even greater heights than you ever could have. That is when people will always remember you—when they follow in your footsteps and emulate what you've built into them, passing on the knowledge and skills as the cycle of multiplication continues. And guess what? Your own legacy, and the impact of your teachings, extends even further, spreading far beyond your own sphere of influence.

Exponential multiplication is a powerful mathematical concept. When creating a liberating legacy, multiplication "to the power of" refers to the idea of multiplying one's efforts and impact in a way that is exponential or geometric rather than linear. This is where you amplify your impact by leveraging relationships, skills, and resources to reach and inspire more people. Every living thing in the world is created to multiply. You are no different. For within you lies a source of pure potentiality, with your spirit yearning to expand.

We are always seeking to be more, do more, have more, give more, and become more as our life is seeking expression of itself.

Ambition, I have come to believe, is the most primal and sacred fundamental of our being, and when it is applied in positive ways that build and create and nurture, its potency is unlimited. Yet ambition alone, without action, is powerless.

To feel ambition and to act upon it is to embrace the unique calling of our souls. Not to act upon that ambition is to turn our backs on ourselves and on the reason for our existence.
—Steven Pressfield

PASS THE BATON

Races are won not so much by the speed of the runner but by the quality of exchanging the baton—from one hand to another.

Legacies are created not by crossing life's finish line; it is by the number of people you prepare to cross that line through the exchange of the baton from one generation to another.

THE WORDS THAT DESCRIBE YOUR LEGACY

What are the words you desire to have associated with your life after you're gone? (Or for that matter, while you're still here?) What will your obituary sound like? Isn't it strange that we so often use such nice words to describe people when they pass on; I say, why wait until then to have great words said about you? Or to say good words about others?

Some years ago, I made an "Affirmation CD," which was eventually distributed to more than 100,000 individuals. Receiving many notes from people who benefited from it, there was one that I always remember—a mother sharing great words with her child.

On the way to school, she would play the CD in the car, thinking her daughter wasn't listening since she seemed uninterested, being more like Chatty Cathy during the ride. Later, the mother was shocked when out of her daughter's mouth one day came the same affirmations. She said her daughter was being bullied at school and the affirmations gave her the confidence she needed to keep going, knowing she was valuable, and not needing the validation of those that put her down.

This is such a wonderful example of how positive words are creating a legacy!

BEING INTENTIONAL

After reading a quote from Trey Smith—"If your presence doesn't make an impact, your absence won't make a difference"—making an impact became more important to me. At that point, I wrote an affirmation, intentionally saying it daily: "I am always working to be in the present and give people my undivided attention." This helped me focus since being present didn't always come naturally for me.

A man I have coached in the past once said to me, "You know, one of the things I'll always remember about you is that we can be at a convention with thousands of people milling around, and when you and I are talking, your eyes don't wander. You're not waiting to move on to the next person. I feel like I'm the only person in the entire room you care about." This showed the power of being intentional, affirming and reminding myself of leaving a legacy I desire to be known for. You can do this too. Write an affirmation around what you desire to be known for.

The only person you are destined to become is the person you decide to be.
—RALPH WALDO EMERSON

What will your rewards look like? Have you thought about what you will contribute to the world? Will people prosper from your accomplishments? Have you or will you build something to leave behind? Is it money you want your legacy to be, or is it more than that? It seems like much of our life, in many places we are known as a number. Social security number, passport number, driver's license number. In my eyes you transcend mere numbers for every number carries a name, every name has a story, and every story matters. You matter and you have a story you desire others to tell after you have passed. What is that story? Have you given any mental energy to creating how that story will be a legacy? What beliefs, values, and perceptions will you pass on?

> *You are not just a number—*
> *for every number has a name,*
> *every name has a story,*
> *and every story matters.*

SHOW AND TELL YOUR LIFE

Did you ever have Show and Tell in school? This was where you were able to bring something to show the class and tell them all about it. One friend of mine, Nicole d'Aquin, brought a frozen, dead shark to school. Really! She was immediately seen as the "cool kid." Yet that shark had to live in her bag *all day*. What do you think happened? By the end of the day, she was not only known for bringing a dead shark to school, she was also known for owning a smelly, disgusting backpack!

There are times in our lives when we think we are the "cool kid" with everything going our way, but if we don't reflect on the choices we have been making, we can become known for what we'd prefer *not* to be! Life is a bit like Show and Tell: You have the opportunity every day to show the world who you are by what you say, what you do, what you have, and what you give.

THE LIFE OF PURPOSE

Viktor Frankl was a Jewish physician trained both in psychiatry and neurology who was practicing in Austria when it came to be occupied by Nazi Germany. He survived three brutal years in various concentration camps, among them Auschwitz. In his book *Man's Search for Meaning*, Frankl discusses the ideas that sustained him during his darkest days.

That sustaining force was the search for purpose as the hallmark of a well-lived life. As Frankl wrote, "Man's main concern is not to gain pleasure or to avoid pain but rather to see a meaning in his life. That is why man is even ready to suffer, on the condition, to be sure, that his suffering has meaning."

Frankl believed this meaning was individual rather than general—every person has to go through the process of discovering meaning for themselves. Now *there* is a prescription for a good life! As Mark Twain said, "The two most important days in your life are the day you are born and the day you find out why."

Under my leadership I had the privilege to work alongside many wonderful coaches. Mark Ramsey was one of them. Knowing that it was important to me to leave a legacy of adding value to others, Mark sent me a video showing that he had kept my teachings going forward, proving that legacy is about multiplying through pouring into one who then pours into others, allowing those teachings to continue to be passed on. In the video, he said,

I am a Christian who has been happily married to Lisa. We have three very successful children. Nicole, our daughter, is now Dr. Nicole Kay Ramsey. She has earned her PhD in Music Education and is a professor at Drake University. Dean is a firefighter for the City of Concord, North Carolina, and Chad is a pilot for PSA Airlines.

I learned so much from you through the programs you wrote, and your principles became transformational for me. Repeating some of your programs more than five times, there was a newfound confidence in me causing me to share with my family what I was learning. We started noticing a culture that coaches under your leadership were living that was different from ours at The Ramsey Group.

At that point in time, I knew I had a lot more to learn. I mustered up the courage to call you directly, and as you spoke you made me feel I was the only person that mattered in your world. I started to see God's bigger picture come into view.

When one chooses to make lifestyle changes, the people around them are affected. That was the case with my wife and children. All but one jumped in 100 percent; the other enjoyed arguing about whether your maxims were correct. Then he chose to join the US Navy. He was allowed to bring only one personal religious item. I was shocked when he brought me his Bible and asked me to write your main principles inside the cover. My suspicions that he had been listening at a different level were confirmed.

As I changed, so did my skills, soon earning a leadership position, and then auditioning to be a coach for you. A childhood dream of speaking, teaching, and helping others through coaching became possible because of that opportunity.

Through this time, I was able to stand in front of and share all I learned with nearly 4,000 agents each year. You also had many other coaches doing the same thing. When you said, "Mark, borrow my belief in you, until you find your own," I knew you meant it. That belief has allowed me to gain my own belief and see greatness in others. May I continue to pass down your legacy.

As you might imagine, Mark's heartfelt message was deeply affirming and encouraging to me. Hearing stories and receiving feedback like that speaks to the purposeful legacy we all can leave. I know you have in you the capability to leave a great one.

CREATING YOUR LEGACY BOOK

Generational Life is a term that describes one generation pouring into a younger one. Take what you have learned and pass it on. Be an example for the next generation to follow.

> *The purpose of life is to discover your gift.*
> *The work of life is to develop it.*
> *The meaning of life is to give your gift away.*
> —David Viscott

My husband and I created a Legacy Book, a three-ring binder where we keep pictures of memorabilia, important papers, and other special items. It even states that when I pass on and the people walk into my memorial, with the pics rotating, there must be popcorn served to every person who attends! Why? So people can celebrate and enjoy while watching the days of our lives! When you prepare your legacy in this way, something happens to you: You become less fearful and more willing to live life to the fullest.

In chapter 5, you were asked to write your eulogy and then condense it to one paragraph or sentence. I asked you to focus on doing whatever you think you have to do to get moving in the direction of fulfilling the life you wrote about. So to close out our journey together, here's a little test: After all the chapters between that first one and this one, have you kept your eye on who it is you chose to become? Have you changed your mind about your legacy or grown beyond what you first wrote?

If not, are you ready to do so now?

I happen to be a person of deep faith, but even if you are not a particularly religious person you can draw incredible freedom from life-crafting a legacy. Start with your head and your heart. Become more and build your legacy today. If you will not imagine it and do it, who will? If not now, when?

> *You can't connect the dots looking forward;*
> *you can only connect them looking backwards.*
> *So you have to trust that the dots*
> *will somehow connect in your future.*
> —STEVE JOBS

May you continue to become more, as there are countless people eagerly anticipating the full expression of your greatness.

There is greatness inside you, can you believe it?

I *do*. Do *you*?

ACKNOWLEDGMENTS

As a child I fell in love with reading books, and to this day I cherish the simple pleasure of curling up on the sofa or down on our boat dock with a good book and a bag of freshly popped kernels from our movie-sized popcorn machine.

One evening, while lost in a book, I received a text from someone thanking me for adding value to their life and asking when I was going to write a book. Though I had been asked the question before, this time it struck a chord. After quickly texting back a thank-you for the kind words and asking how they were doing, I went back to reading. There in front of me was a quote of John F. Kennedy's: "If not us, who? If not now, when?" That was the final nudge I needed to embark on the journey of becoming an author.

I am filled with deep gratitude and appreciation for the incredible individuals who have played a pivotal and instrumental role in helping me bring this book to life. First and foremost, I want to thank my beloved husband, Tony, whose unwavering support and belief in me has been the driving force behind this project. I am eternally grateful for your love.

To my children and immediate family, Shon, Rosy, Shane, and Todd—as well as Cherie Starke and Cindy Nelson, who lived with me for a few years while their mother was ill—and my grandchildren Jacqueline, Armando, Dante, and Marybella—thank you for being a constant source of love and inspiration.

ACKNOWLEDGMENTS

In remembrance of my parents, Sam and Bette Colobella, I would like to pay tribute to them for instilling in me great values such as devotion to family, determination, achievement, and encouraging others. Through their guidance, they taught me the importance of giving back. Equally significant is that they opened doors for me to learn from exceptional thought leaders such as Zig Ziglar, Norman Vincent Peale, Og Mandino, Robert Schuller, and numerous others. I hold their memory dear.

My sincere appreciation to Don Yaeger for his guidance on what it takes to write a book and to Jeffery S. Lindsay, Kaitlyn Merchant Davison, Dave Moore, and Nicole d'Aquin for your contribution and support. Nicole, your ability to bring to life the models I sketched on napkins and scrap paper is unmatched. I want to thank Stephanie Thomas for stepping in at the last minute to help during crunch time. A special thank-you to Ryan Peter for your attention to detail in helping edit my writing; your expertise and dedication were instrumental.

To the leadership of Mark Cole, CEO of the John Maxwell Company, to my editor Phil Newman, and to the excellent team at Forefront Books—Jonathan Merkh, Justin Batt, Jen Gingerich, and Billie Brownell—thank you for journeying with me from the initial manuscript all the way to this amazing final product.

A big shout-out to the talented and skilled doctors who have helped me on my journey of personal growth, allowing me to ask questions and reassuring me that what I wrote was medically sound. Dr. Shane Kokoszka, Dr. Damon Whitfield, and Dr. Eleanor Womack, your guidance and expertise have been invaluable.

My sincere gratitude to Gary Keller, the visionary founder of Keller Williams Realty International, for the opportunity to build and lead the highly acclaimed MAPS Coaching and Training

ACKNOWLEDGMENTS

Company as CEO. To Mary Tennant, President of KWRI, who entrusted me with the task of writing a training program based on insights from my personal journals. This program known as BOLD (Business Objective: A Life by Design) has had a profound impact on numerous lives, and the overwhelming response from BOLD attendees has motivated and even implored me to embark on writing this book. Thank you all for your unwavering support and enthusiasm.

Heartfelt appreciation for my mentor, John C. Maxwell, who challenged me to think bigger by providing me with unparalleled experiences. Thank you for allowing me to become more by traveling with you and your team, meeting presidents and prime ministers, teaching values and bringing transformation to their nations.

Thanks to my wonderful sister, Raelene Davis, who read and reread the manuscript with meticulous detail, always willing to help. To Ashley Lunn and Brenda Dashner, for offering feedback and encouragement.

Erin Miller, your knowledgeable insights on writing styles and wisdom were truly priceless. Thanks also to Hannah Sutton for presenting the younger generation's viewpoint.

To Paige LoPinto and Melissa Jimenez for helping me with the household and scheduling so I could focus on the book, travel, and health issues.

And to my loyal friends who continue to call me and cheer me on.

Without the support and guidance of these incredible individuals, this book would not have been possible. Thank you, all of you, from the bottom of my heart.

ADDITIONAL RESOURCES

"3 Ways Your Beliefs Can Shape Your Reality," *Psychology Today*, Retrieved May 18, 2023, https://www.psychologytoday.com/us/blog/in-love-and-war/201508/3-ways -your-beliefs-can-shape-your-reality.

"Acceptance and Commitment Therapy," *Psychology Today*, Retrieved May 18, 2023, https://www.psychologytoday.com/us/therapy-types/acceptance-and -commitment-therapy.

Adelphi Psych Medicine Clinic, https://adelphipsych.sg/author/joeihuangkanza.

Amen MD, Daniel G., *Your Brain Is Always Listening* (Tyndale, 2021).

Morin, A., "Cognitive Reframing: Definition, Techniques, Efficacy," Verywell Mind, March 23, 2011, https://www.verywellmind.com/reframing -defined-2610419.

Huberman, Andrew, bio, Retrieved May 18, 2023, https://drive .google.com/file/d/1ekQFe2TK8LC_K8U1VnvsaVNhjxyIQOLi/view.

Shiba, K., et al., "Associations between Purpose in Life and Mortality by SES," *American Journal of Preventive Medicine* 61, no. 2 (2021): e53-e61, https://pubmed.ncbi.nlm.nih.gov/34020851/.

Feldman Barrett, L., *How Emotions Are Made* (HarperCollins, 2017).

Bikman, B., *Why We Get Sick: The Hidden Epidemic at the Root of Most Chronic Disease—and How to Fight It* (BenBella Books, 2020).

Brackett, M., *Permission to Feel* (Celadon, 2020).

Burston, C., "How to Change Mindset and Attitude: 14 Tips to Change Your Life," https://chrisburston.com/how-to-change-mindset-and-attitude/.

ADDITIONAL RESOURCES

Buzan, T., *Mind Maps at Work* (Penguin, 2005).

"Carl Rogers' Humanistic Theory of Personality Development," Simply Psychology, November 3, 2022, https://www.simplypsychology.org/carl-rogers.html.

Chopra, D., & Tanzi, R., *Super Genes* (Harmony, 2017).

Christakis, N. A., & Fowler, J. H., "The Spread of Obesity in a Large Social Network over 32 Years," *The New England Journal of Medicine*, 2007, https://doi.org/10.1056/NEJMsa066082.

Cialdini, R. B., "Energy Conservation: A Social Influence Perspective," *Personality and Social Psychology Bulletin* vol. 13 (1987): 309–18.

Cloud, H., & Townsend, J., *Boundaries* (Grand Rapids, MI: Zondervan, 2008).

"Codependency," *Psychology Today*, Retrieved May 18, 2023, https://www.psychologytoday.com/us/basics/codependency.

Cole, S., Riccio, M., & Balcetis, E., "Focused and Fired Up: Narrowed Attention Produces Perceived Proximity and Increases Goal-Relevant Action," *Motivation and Emotion*, 6, 2014: 815–22, https://doi.org/10.1007/s11031-014-9432-3.

Crum, A., "Change Your Mindset, Change the Game," TEDxTraverseCity, YouTube, October 15, 2014, https://www.youtube.com/watch?v=0tqq66zwa7g.

Crum, A. (n.d.), "Harnessing The Power of Placebos," TEDMED, Retrieved May 18, 2023, https://www.tedmed.com/talks/show?id=621415.

Daniels, M. E., *100 Days of Believing Bigger* (Dayspring, 2020).

Eagleman, D., bio, Retrieved May 18, 2023, https://drive.google.com/file/d/1hpA17JcRgNIxTN9uVopdAJ7ribTogBlf/view.

David, S. *Emotional Agility* (Penguin, 2016).

Debanne, D., Campanac, E., Bialowas, A., Carlier, E., & Alcaraz, G., "Axon Physiology," *Physiological Reviews*, 2 (2011): 555–602, https://doi.org/10.1152/physrev.00048.2009.

"Do Narcissists Know They Are Narcissists?" *Psychology Today*, Retrieved May 18, 2023, https://www.psychologytoday.com/us/blog/beautiful-minds/201103/do-narcissists-know-they-are-narcissists.

Donaldson-Pressman, S., Pressman, R. M., & Pressman, R. H., *The Narcissistic Family* (Jossey-Bass, 1994).

ADDITIONAL RESOURCES

Eagleman, D., *The Brain with David Eagleman*, PBS, Retrieved May 18, 2023, https://www.pbs.org/show/brain-david-eagleman/.

"Emotional Agility," *Harvard Business Review*, November 1, 2013, https://hbr.org/2013/11/emotional-agility.

Ghosh, R., et al., "Exposure to Sound Vibrations Lead to Transcriptomic, Proteomic and Hormonal Changes in Arabidopsis," *Scientific Reports* 6 (2016), https://www.nature.com/articles/srep33370.

Fredrickson, B. L., et al., "A Functional Genomic Perspective on Human Well-Being," *Proceedings of the National Academy of Sciences* 33 (2013): 13684–89, https://doi.org/10.1073/pnas.1305419110.

Gelb, M. J., *Discover Your Genius* (HarperCollins, 2009).

Gelb, M. J., *How to Think like Leonardo da Vinci* (Dell, 2009).

Hall, N., *Change Your Beliefs, Change Your Life: How to Take Control, Break Old Habits, and Live the Life You Deserve* (Nightingale - Conant, 2000).

Hammond, D. J., *The Fine Art of Doing Better* (American Motivational Association, 1974).

Huberman, A., "The Genius Life: 83: How to Instantly De-Stress and Supplement for Better Health, Sleep, and Longevity," December 11, 2019, https://thegeniuslife.libsyn.com/83-how-to-instantly-de-stress-and-supplements-for-better-health-sleep-and-longevity-andrew-huberman-phd.

"Is Purpose in Life Associated with Less Sleep Disturbance in Older Adults?" Sleep Science and Practice, Retrieved May 18, 2023, https://sleep.biomedcentral.com/articles/10.1186/s41606-017-0015-6.

Kendall, R. T., *Fear* (Charisma Media, 2022).

Kerr, F., Malcolm, L., Dean, D., & Shabunov, A. "Look Up and Connect," ABC Radio National, https://www.abc.net.au/radionational/programs/allinthemind/look-up-and-connect/11823040.

Kirova, D., "What Are Core Values, and Why Are They Important?" Values Institute, Retrieved May 18, 2023, https://values.institute/what-are-core-values-and-why-are-they-important/.

Kolata, G., "Obesity Spreads to Friends, Study Concludes," *New York Times*, July 25, 2007, https://www.nytimes.com/2007/07/25/health/25iht-fat.4.6830240.html.

ADDITIONAL RESOURCES

Leonard, J. A., Garcia, A., & Schulz, L. E., "How Adults' Actions, Outcomes, and Testimony Affect Preschoolers' Persistence," *Child Development* 4 (2019): 1254–71, https://doi.org/10.1111/cdev.13305.

Schippers, M. C., & Ziegler, N., "Life Crafting as a Way to Find Purpose and Meaning in Life," *Frontiers in Psychology* 10 (2019): 2778, https://pubmed.ncbi.nlm.nih.gov/31920827/.

Locke, R. "The Stories of These 5 Athletes Will Motivate Every One of You," Lifehack, https://www.lifehack.org/articles/communication/the-stories-these-5-athletes-will-motivate-everyone-you.html.

Loehr, J. E., & McLaughlin, P. J., *Mental Toughness Training: Commanding the Ideal Performance State at Will* (Nightingale - Conant, 1990).

Manson, M., *The Subtle Art of Not Giving a F*ck* (HarperCollins, 2016).

Martin, D., *Mindset Matters* (Avail, 2021).

McGonigal, K., "How To Make Stress Your Friend," TED Talk, September 4, 2013, https://www.ted.com/talks/kelly_mcgonigal_how_to_make_stress_your_friend/c.

Medina, J., *Brain Rules,* updated and expanded (Pear Press, 2014).

"Mindsets," The Peak Performance Center, Retrieved May 18, 2023, https://thepeakperformancecenter.com/development-series/mental-conditioning/mindsets/.

Nelson, B., *The Emotion Code* (St. Martin's Essentials, 2019).

Kaplin, A., & Anzaldi, L., "New Movement in Neuroscience: A Purpose-Driven Life," *Cerebrum* (2015), https://www.ncbi.nlm.nih.gov/pmc/articles/PMC4564234/.

Newberg, A., & Waldman, M. R., *Words Can Change Your Brain* (Penguin, 2013).

Celestine, N., "How to Change Self-Limiting Beliefs According to Psychology," PositivePsychology.com, November 24, 2015, https://positivepsychology.com/false-beliefs/.

"Oxford Word of the Year 2016," Oxford Languages, Retrieved May 18, 2023, https://languages.oup.com/word-of-the-year/2016/.

Pagel, M., "How Language Transformed Humanity," TED Talk, August 3, 2011, https://www.ted.com/talks/mark_pagel_how_language_transformed_humanity?referrer=playlist-how_language_changes_over_time&autoplay=true.

ADDITIONAL RESOURCES

"Personal Core Values List: 569 Scientific and Inspirational Examples," Focality, Retrieved May 18, 2023, https://www.focalityapp.com/en/resources/personal-core-values-list/.

Petronis, A., & Labrie, V., "The Crossroads of Psychiatric Epigenomics," *World Psychiatry* 3 (2019): 353–54, https://doi.org/10.1002/wps.20675.

Scott, E., "Cognitive Distortions and Stress," Verywell Mind, November 29, 2007, https://www.verywellmind.com/cognitive-distortions-and-stress-3144921.

Pink, D. H., *A Whole New Mind* (Penguin, 2006).

Positive Psychology Center, Retrieved May 18, 2023, https://ppc.sas.upenn.edu/.

Price, D., "An Explorer's Guide to Epigenetics," *Brain World*, December 9, 2017, https://brainworldmagazine.com/explorers-guide-epigenetics/.

Ptak, C., & Petronis, A., "Epigenetic Approaches to Psychiatric Disorders," *Dialogues in Clinical Neuroscience* 1 (2010): 25–35, https://doi.org/10.31887/dcns.2010.12.1/cptak.

Zilioli, S., et al., "Purpose in Life Predicts Allostatic Load Ten Years Later," *Journal of Psychosomatic Research* 79, no. 5 (2015): 451-57, https://pubmed.ncbi.nlm.nih.gov/26526322/.

Ree, L. I., *Understanding Human Emotions* (2021).

"U.S. Behavioral Health Market Size to Worth Around US$," GlobeNewswire, November 10, 2021 https://www.globenewswire.com/news-release/2021/11/10/2331828/0/en/U-S-Behavioral-Health-Market-Size-to-Worth-Around-US-132-4-Bn-by-2027.html.

Robinson, A., "8.1: Build Your Superpower," January 19, 2021, https://buildyoursuperpower.substack.com/p/81-build-your-superpower-adam-robinson#details.

Rokeach, M., *Beliefs, Attitudes, and Values* (Jossey-Bass Inc. Pub, 1968).

Rokeach, M., *The Nature of Human Values* (Free Press, 1973).

Sigman, M., "Your Words May Predict Your Future Mental Health," TED Talk, May 24, 2016, https://www.ted.com/talks/mariano_sigman_your_words_may_predict_your_future_mental_health?language=ky&subtitle=en.

Sisters, A., "Epigenetics," YouTube, December 18, 2020, https://www.youtube.com/watch?v=MD3Fc0XOjWk.

Snyder, M., "Everything Is F*cked," Thrice Removed, March 18, 2020, https://medium.com/thrice-removed/everything-is-f-cked-5a7660a4856.

ADDITIONAL RESOURCES

Spiegel, A., "Why Even Radiologists Can Miss a Gorilla Hiding in Plain Sight," NPR, February 11, 2013, https://www.npr.org/sections/health-shots/2013/02/11/171409656/why-even-radiologists-can-miss-a-gorilla-hiding-in-plain-sight/.

"'You've Got to Find What You Love,' Jobs says," Stanford News, June 12, 2005, https://news.stanford.edu/2005/06/12/youve-got-find-love-jobs-says/.

Steptoe, A., Deaton, A., & Stone, A. A., "Subjective Wellbeing, Health, and Ageing," *The Lancet* 9968 (2014): 640–48, https://doi.org/https://doi.org/10.1016/S0140-6736(13)61489-0.

Capaldi, F. R., et al., "Sulfur Metabolism and Stress Defense Responses in Plants," *Tropical Plant Biology* 8 (2015): 60-73, https://link.springer.com/article/10.1007/s12042-015-9152-1.

Tanzi, R. E., & Chopra, D., *Super Brain* (Harmony, 2013).

Taylor, S. A., *Quantum Success* (National Geographic Books, 2006).

Guerrero-Bosagna, C., "What Is Epigenetics?" June 27, 2016, YouTube, https://www.youtube.com/watch?v=_aAhcNjmvhc.

The Last Dance, ESPN, 2020, https://www.imdb.com/title/tt8420184/.

"*The Power of the Placebo Effect,*" Harvard Health., https://www.health.harvard.edu/mental-health/the-power-of-the-placebo-effect.

"Values: Schwartz Theory of Basic Values—Relocated," Australian National University, Retrieved May 18, 2023. https://i2s.anu.edu.au/resources/schwartz-theory-basic-values.

Walton, A. G., "The Science of Giving Back: How Having a Purpose Is Good for Body and Brain," *Forbes*, July 10, 2017, https://www.forbes.com/sites/alicegwalton/2017/07/10/the-science-of-giving-back-how-having-a-purpose-is-good-for-body-and-brain/?sh=5f4a1d2a6146.

"Why Saying Is Believing—The Science of Self-Talk," NPR, October 7, 2014, https://www.npr.org/transcripts/353292408.

Yeager, D. S., et al., "Breaking the Cycle of Mistrust: Wise Interventions to Provide Critical Feedback Across the Racial Divide," *Journal of Experimental Psychology: General* 2 (2014): 804–824, https://doi.org/10.1037/a0033906.

Zimmer, C. "The Famine Ended 70 Years Ago, but Dutch Genes Still Bear Scars," January 31, 2018, *New York Times,* nytimes.com/2018/01/31/science/dutch-famine-genes.html.

ABOUT
THE AUTHOR

Dianna Kokoszka is an entrepreneur, keynote speaker, author, and mentor. As an award-winning business leader, she has established herself as a prominent figure in the business world, developing many leaders during her long career. Dedicating thirteen years as CEO of KW MAPS Coaching and Training at Keller Williams Realty International, she played a pivotal role in propelling the company to become the largest and most profitable coaching enterprise in the real estate industry. As innovator, creator, and author of the KW BOLD Experience and Coaching Skills Camp, she helped lead the company to be recognized as the number one training company in the world.

She is a board member of Growing Leaders, a Maxwell Leadership Foundation organization, and captures every opportunity to journey alongside EQUIP Leadership Inc., a nonprofit dedicated to instilling values in individuals and transforming nations.

Dianna is a certified practitioner of Neuro-Linguistic Programing (NLP), a founding member of the John Maxwell Team of Certified Coaches (IMC), and an active participant in the Strategic Coach training program. A lifelong learner, she has followed and been mentored by John C. Maxwell since the mid-1990s. Her greatest passions revolve around developing leaders and encouraging

ABOUT THE AUTHOR

individuals to recognize and harness their innate potential.

Among her impressive achievements, Dianna's most cherished titles are wife, mother, and grandmother. Her genuine concern for the welfare of others serves as the driving force behind all her endeavors, fueling her unwavering commitment to add value to others.